Homewrecker

AN ADULTERY READER

Edited by Daphne Gottlieb

© 2005 Daphne Gottlieb

Cover and interior design by Gary Fogelson

Published by Soft Skull Press
55 Washington Street, Suite 804
Brooklyn, NY 11201

Distributed by Publishers Group West
800.788.3123 | www.pgw.com

Printed in Canada

Library of Congress Cataloging-in-Publication Data

Homewrecker : an adultery reader / edited by Daphne Gottlieb.
    p. cm.
Includes bibliographical references.
ISBN 1-932360-93-X (alk. paper)
1. Adultery—Literary collections. 2. American literature.
I. Gottlieb, Daphne, 1968–
PS509.A29H66 2005
810.8'3552—dc22
                                                2005004295

CONTENTS

for Tennessee Jones

LET'S JUST GET THIS OUT IN THE OPEN

Daphne Gottlieb

I was fourteen and madly in love for the first time. He was twenty-one. He made me suddenly, unaccustomedly beautiful with his kisses and mix tapes. During the year of elation and longing, he never mentioned that he had a girlfriend who lived across the street. A serious girl. A girl his age. A girl he loved. Unlike inappropriate, high school, secret me.

The next time, I was fifteen and visiting a friend at college. It was a friend's friend's boyfriend who looked like Jim Morrison and wore leather pants and burned candles and incense. His girlfriend was at work and I wanted him to touch me. She found out. I don't know what happened after that.

I was nineteen and he was my boyfriend's archrival. I was twenty and it was my lover's girlfriend and we had to lie because otherwise he always wanted to watch. I was twenty-four and her girlfriend knew about it but then changed her mind about the open relationship. We saw each other anyway. I was thirty when we met—we wanted each other but were committed to other people; the way we look at each other still scorches the walls. I turned thirty-something and pointedly wasn't invited to a funeral/a wedding/a baby shower because of a rumor.

I am a few years older now and I know this: There are tastes of mouths I could not have lived without; there are times I've pretended it was just about the sex because I couldn't stand the way my heart was about to burst with happiness and awe and I couldn't be that vulnerable, not again, not with this one. That waiting to have someone's stolen seconds can burn you alive. That the shittiest thing you can do in the world is lie to someone you love; also that there are certain times you have no other choice—not honoring this fascination, this car crash of desire, is also a lie. That there is power in having someone risk everything for you. That there is nothing more frightening than being willing to take this freefall. That it is not as simple as we were always promised. Love— at least the pair-bonded, prescribed love—does not conquer all. It does not conquer desire.

Arrow, meet heart. Apple, meet Eve.

If it's an old story, it's an endlessly compelling one that we can't stop telling, in the headlines and on Jerry Springer, from politics to pornography. But if these conversations are happening out there in mass culture, they also occur in the quietest and most painful ways in our own homes. And there's no doubt these conversations are happening, even though statistics vary widely, from a marginal 15 percent to a whopping 80 percent of married couples cheating. Perhaps it's true in the public perception that, as a close single male friend said, "Monogamy is what you can get away with." But if there are so many people straying outside the lines, maybe it's time to examine how we really love—maybe then we'll be able to talk about adultery without snickering, whispering, or screaming.

After *Homewrecker*'s call for submissions went out, I received a number of fevered, upset emails. Over and over, they said: *You're not in FAVOR of it, are you?* I want to believe (but rather doubt) that this same question would be asked of me as the editor of an anthology on motherhood, cancer, or swing dance. But mothers, the ill, and dancers do not have to lie to nurture, heal, or perform. (On a side note, if cheating is as rampant as even the moderate statistics suggest, it strikes me as odd that we're still blaming the "homewrecker" rather than questioning the system. What would it look like if we prized honesty and love instead of pair fidelity?)

As a writer, I'm drawn to contradiction and cataclysm, compelled by ambivalent, tortured emotional states. As a feminist, I'm appalled that most of the acculturated stories we have about adultery end with the betraying, sinister woman being punished/cast out while adulterous men come back, transformed, renewed, rescued. As an American queer, I'm on the outside of the primary happily-ever-after story we tell about Love, and over and over I'm struck by how hard-won this myth and its unlikely actualization are—for anyone.

Here then, I hope, are stories, poems, and essays about the way it really breaks down, about what desire does to us, about what happens when we're incandescent but are not allowed to be, about what we look like when we adore, and, in the end, what it costs.

HOW TO HAVE AN AFFAIR
Michael Hemmingson

The Rules

Wait at least an hour, maybe two, for your wife to fall sleep before going out to see the other woman. The wife usually hits the bed around 10 or 11 PM; she has to get up early and work at the office. She adjusted her life years ago to your nocturnal habits; you like to work at night behind the computer, writing genre novels (westerns, action-adventure) for book packagers under various "house names." Because your wife sleeps, as they say, like the dead, it's easy for you to slip out of the house for a few hours, return at two or three in the morning. She never has a clue you've been gone.

When you're certain the wife is quite asleep, call the other woman on her cell phone. The other woman's husband is a doctor so he's often away, and that marriage is strained as it is. She keeps saying she'll leave him. She waits impatiently for your call. "God, I need to see you bad," she says.

There are two ways you meet her, depending on how much time she has: (1) She'll drive her car over, park a block away, you'll walk to her car, and the two of you will do your affair thing quickly in the back seat like a couple of kids sneaking sex in the dangerous night; or (2) you will walk three blocks to a cheap motel by the freeway on-ramp, call her cell and inform her of the room number, and engage in some quality hours. Either way, you return home, the wife hasn't stirred, you get some work done, you go to sleep around four or five in the morning; you sleep like the dead yourself when the wife gets up at 7:30 to shower, dress, and make way for the office.

This goes on for six months or so; you never get caught but there's always that possibility, that thrill. You could lose everything here. Your wife would leave you in the dust if she ever found out.

The other woman really doesn't care if her husband, the doctor, ever finds out.

"I'm not in love anymore, what does it matter," she says.

"He'd be hurt."

"I don't think so. Maybe I should tell him."

"No," you say. "Don't tell him."

"You're right," she says. "I do want some money when the time comes for a divorce."

I Don't Ever Want to See You Again

The other woman eventually leaves the doctor and rents an apartment five blocks from your house. It makes things easier for a while, but after a month she lets you know she really wishes you could spend the night. "I want to wake up with you in my bed," she says. This just is not possible. You try getting up after your wife goes to work and returning to the other woman's apartment, but this is simply exhausting. The other woman is worried you have sex with your wife the same nights you have sex with her. "That's crazy," you say, although you have committed this sin on several occasions because, let's face it, you're a bad man.

One night, the other woman expresses her dislike at being the mistress, although you've never thought of her as such, and asks: "Do you love me?"

"I love my wife, I can't love two—"

"Get out!" she says. "I don't ever want to see you again."

It's raining. You feel terrible. You do love her, so you call her from a pay phone and, dripping wet, are prepared to tell the other woman that you're scared because you love two women with equal passion and could there ever be a true future in that, but the other woman doesn't give you a chance to bare your ugly soul, she says: "Come back. I don't care if you don't love me, I love you, I need you, it's really all about sex, right? The sex is good so come back and fuck me, okay?"

Scent of the Other Woman

In time, you get caught; anyone who ever has an affair for an extended period will eventually be caught. One night you come home at three in the morning and your wife is awake, sitting on the couch and drinking a drink.

"Oh," you say.

"Where have you been?" she says.

"I—I went out for a walk," you say, "I needed to clear my head."

"You've been gone since eleven," she says.

"It was a long walk," you say.

"I followed you," she says. "You thought I was asleep. My eyes were closed, yes, but I was not asleep. When you left five hours ago, I followed you to an apartment building. Who is she?"

"Look," you say, but you know it's over and there's no way of talking yourself out of this.

"I can smell her on you," says your wife. "I've been smelling her for a while. I thought I was imagining it. I thought I was crazy. But this has been going on for some time now, hasn't it? I should've seen it. How long has this been going on?"

"A while."

"A month?"

"A year."

"A year?"

"Yeah."

"You bastard."

"I'm sorry."

"Who is she?"

You tell her.

"Oh," your wife says. "Oh, I know her. Yes, of course. Why did you choose her?"

"I don't know."

"You have a week," says your wife, "the end of the week to have all your stuff out of this house. Then we'll talk lawyers."

"Be reasonable," you say.

"I am," she says. "I could kick you out right now."

Next: Write Poetry

You move in with the other woman and she's happy about this change. Now you can sleep in her bed. She's now a girlfriend, the significant other. Her divorce is finalized and she talks about a second marriage, when your divorce goes through. Her apartment is too small so you both rent a condo. Your divorce proceedings begin. It's hard to work on the genre novels so you work on a screenplay but your agent says, "Everyone writes those things and they're not as easy to sell as you might think; you might as well write poetry." So you start to write poetry.

Your girlfriend is not the other woman, the sex is no longer exhilarating and perilous. She seems bored with you as well. You flirt with her friends, hoping something might happen, and she doesn't appreciate this one bit. "Has it always been like this with you," she asks, "is there always a wife or girlfriend and another woman?

"No," you say, and soon find yourself in a one-bedroom apartment. Your divorce is finalized and you're single.

The Rules of Being Single

You don't like being single, you have no idea how to be single. You hate sleeping alone; it's so damn lonely. You don't know how to meet women and you've never been comfortable asking them out on dates. You suggest to your ex-wife something about trying it all over again, from scratch, but she says, "I'm seeing someone and I'm in love." You're still friends with an ex-girlfriend from ten years ago and while she's willing to go out to dinner and such with you, to drink and talk and whatnot, she's not interested in a relationship. "You're not easy to be with," she says.

At a party, you meet a friend of this ex-girlfriend's that you feel is attracted to you. You're attracted to her. She's married but you know she's not happy, she's looking for something. You talk to her on the phone a few times but she says she can't see you, she's married. Two months later, she calls and says, "I'm separated now, I have my own apartment, I can go out on dates. I haven't gone out on a date in thirteen years."

After the first date is through, she shakes your hand, she does-n't invite you in, she says, "That was fun; let's do it again."

Max Rod

On the second date with this woman, you go to a restaurant she says is her favorite. At the bar, waiting for a table, she runs into a married couple she knows. The couple look at you like you're a child molester.

"They don't know I'm separated," she tells you later. "So imagine their surprise when they see me with you. They thought I was having an affair!" she says with delight.

"Did you ever have an affair while you were married?"

"I had a one-night stand. It was at a conference—different city, a big hotel on the waterfront in the middle of summer. He was mar-ried, we were both attracted to each other. I felt guilty when I went home. I felt guilty for months. I told myself I'd never do that again, and I didn't."

She's quite interested in your affair story—she finds it exciting. "I have such a dreadfully uneventful life," she says. She wants all the details from you, especially about the sex. And you're good with the minutiae because you are presently writing porn novels under the name "Max Rod" for a book packager to pay the rent.

"So where are they now?" she asks.

You say, "My ex-wife is pregnant and is getting remarried; my ex-girlfriend is robbing the cradle—she's dating a nineteen-year-old college student."

"I would've never been good at it," the woman on the date says, "having an affair. Seems too complicated."

"It's easy when you're doing it," you say, "complex in theory."

HOW TO COMMIT ADULTERY

David A. Hernandez

Exhume your heart. Put the bleeding thing
inside a Ziploc, inside the freezer.
Pocket your wedding band and drive

to the nearest bar. Have a drink.
Have another. Make conversation
with the woman with fishnet stockings

mapping the topography of her legs.
Be charming. Say *A blind man
could fall in love with your eyes.*

Say *I want to memorize the alphabet
of your body.* Have one more drink
at her apartment. Compliment her

on the décor, the zebra-striped couch,
the lava lamp in the corner of her bedroom
juggling its organs in slow motion.

Kiss. Unclasp her bra, unloosen your belt,
varnish her skin with your tongue.
Do what you came there to do.

Get dressed, go home, pretend nothing
happened. When your wife finds it
in the freezer the morning after,

when she asks *What is this?*, say *Dinner.*
Let it thaw all day on the kitchen counter.
Listen to it shushing on the grill.

THE BUSINESS OF LEAVING

Felicia Sullivan

James leans against the railing outside the subway station in Chinatown, watching his two children weave in and out of stores on Mott and Kenmare streets. He rehearses a speech in his mind. Boxes—dozens crowd the narrow sidewalks; knock-off designer purses wrapped in wrinkled plastic sit on a crushed display. Familiar logos are stamped on pleather. Short men with frayed belts buckled tight, stomachs spilling over their slacks, point to the colorful display of perfume bottles. Nearby, he sees his daughter Gillian smile at the men. A sliver of tongue pokes out from her lips. The men shiver in thick, black down coats from the morning chill. The streets smell of Joy and White Diamonds mixed with fresh catch. In the outdoor markets that line the street, fresh fish swim in dirty white buckets. His son, Bunny, pauses in front of a store and eyes today's catch.

James concentrates on memorizing the index cards. In the event that he forgets anything, he has these colored cards as a point of reference. He wants to incorporate phrases such as, "Be strong for your mother" (blue index card for Strength) and "My leaving really doesn't change anything" (white index card for Closing Comments) into his speech.

He imagines Gillian's eyes narrowing into a condescending glare when he tells her he is leaving their family for another woman. Perhaps she will give him the silent treatment, refuse him the satisfaction of her caring about what he has done to them. He could escape unscathed and rush back to his Cadillac, parked at Syosset train station; his life packed into two large duffel bags that sit in the trunk. James always falls apart when he argues with his wife and his daughter.

Among the dark suits and toiletries that he packed is a picture of his son Bunny—the only picture he took from the stack of photo albums lodged in their living room bookcase. Bunny was three in the photo. Nibbling on a large blade of grass with his one hand, he was giving James the middle finger with the other. Gillian had stood blurred in the background; however, James could remember her running over to Bunny and folding all but one of his fingers down. Scurrying away, she had shouted, "Cheese!" as James snapped the photo. While Gillian marched about the lawn giving James Nazi salutes, Emma had stood in the background smothering a chuckle. After James had lowered the camera to his waist, he wondered what he had ever done to deserve this—an angry daughter, a cold wife and a beautiful son caught in the middle of all of this anger.

He knows his fragile son, who is most comfortable hiding in cabinets and under tables draped with linen, won't be able to handle the news. Imagine if he told Bunny that this woman was not the first. The same hand that ruffles his son's head has stroked the insides of soft thighs. James will watch his son cry. Biting his lip, James knows he will crush a smaller version of himself.

Go back to the cards.

Blinking away all of these images, James grips the cards with two fingers. Having spent a miserable seventeen years with his wife, he wants to make a clean break. Within the last two years of their marriage, Emma had grown solemn. She left dishes in the dishwasher for days; her once creatively packed lunches (which contained little cartoon clippings and heart-shaped cupcakes) now comprised leftovers in Tupperware. James wondered if she had grown listless because her children were going to school, tying their own shoes, and brushing their own hair. Her presence was merely a technicality. She made guest appearances at PTA functions and after-school activities that her children would have chosen. They chose none. A year ago, Emma and James had quietly seen a therapist. After the single session, his wife had shuddered, "I don't think that this is right for me." James had asked, "Is it me?" Emma turned to him; her eyes seemed to glare past him. "No, it's me. Does that make you feel better?" From that evening on, she slept with her back facing him, her body on the very edge of the bed. She draped herself in a separate set of sheets. James stopped caring.

James sees Bunny reach inside a blue bucket. Snatching a tiny black eel into his coat pocket, he wipes his oil-glossed hand on the sides of his black coat. Standing idle, he whistles out of tune. The eel slaps against Bunny's waist. He pats the fish gently, "Ssh!" James covers his eyes with his hands, every so often widening two fingers.

James studies the index cards. He struggles not to run up to his son and pull the fish from his coat. Be strong, he tells himself.

Gillian is smoothing Chanel No. 5 on the cracks of her elbows and purrs "Smell" to a thin, pale-faced man. A few feet from James, the man leans to one side, slurping on a small cup of coffee. Grime forms half crescents under his fingernails. "Nice," he spits through pink, fleshy lips. Gillian stares at him; her green eyes widen. The man's two front teeth hang like loose shingles and his bottom teeth converge inward. James sees his daughter lick her thin lips and pout. Pulling a twenty from her wallet she says, "Keep the change." Skipping up and down Canal Street, Gillian sprays Chanel No. 5 in the air, blinding passersby.

At the train station, James's fatigue-green khakis block the green circular number six sign. He begins to shake his leg, irritated. He hides his cards in his coat pocket. As his daughter nears, his face folds—eyes begin to tear; his cheeks cave. James pulls at his wool scarf and wraps it several times around his face. Only his eyes are visible. Through the thin holes in the material, he shouts, "You smell like your mother!" Gillian presses her forefinger down on the nozzle and a mist of lavender and powder surrounds James.

"I know," she says. Gillian unzips her cardigan and her nipples, small raspberry pearls, poke through her tight, see-through tank. James stifles a nervous laugh and wonders if he has ever loved his daughter.

When Gillian was fourteen, James came home early from work to find her at the kitchen counter pouring water into a bottle of vodka. The home held its familiar astringent perfumes: Lysol, alcohol, disinfectant—he felt as if he stepped inside an airplane. Next to the bottle of vodka stood a tall glass of orange juice; pulp had floated to the top. The new Polaroid camera James had bought Gillian for her birthday sat on the kitchen table. Pictures scattered the counter. Staring at the photographs, she raised the glass to her lips and in several gulps finished the drink then poured another. Spreading the photos in the shape of a rainbow, she spat at them. James watched her hands rove the photos. He saw her bend and curl a few under her palm. Enough, he thought. Stomping over,

James tore the glass from Gillian's hands and threw it in the sink. Glass flew about the kitchen: on the table, pieces landed on the floor, bits got caught in her hair. His wife Emma slithered down the stairs in a periwinkle terry robe and draped one hand onto the doorway panel. Her skin was clear and firm with a bluish pallor, a film negative. Through glazed eyes, she took in the scene: the shattered glass, her petulant daughter, and James. Exhaling, she balanced herself against the doorway.

"Rough day with Valium, dear?" James shouted, tightening his slate gray tie around his neck, hoping to black out, to not see his fourteen-year-old daughter guzzling mid-day cocktails. "Look at all this mess," he said in disgust, sweeping his hand about the room.

"Like you didn't create it," Gillian said.

James saw Bunny huddled in the corner of the kitchen. Smiling weakly, he said, "Bunny, go play."

Gillian reached out for Bunny, spread her arms wide. "Come," she begged.

Bunny sat frozen.

"Why all the shouting?" Chunks of Emma's hair scratched her shoulders like stiff bristles. Dark brown roots bled into blonde highlights. Gillian stacked the photos on the counter and began to shuffle them in her hands like cards. But then she paused at one picture, pressed her thumb hard against the glossy paper and then brought it to her lips. James started to sweat.

"You threw a glass," Gillian whispered, walking towards her mother. Parsing out a tiny shard, she said, "James, it's in my hair."

Emma combed her fingers through chunks of dyed pink tendrils and tightly curled the pieces under her fingers like an umbilical cord. James scowled. When she was a toddler, he had tried to cradle Gillian in his arms, but she had fought him, pressing her tiny pink palms against his neck, her face turning a blistering red. Instead, she had always reached for her mother. Gillian hated him, James had thought, even then.

"Stop calling me James!" he replied. James turned to his wife, who had started to nod off, "And your daughter was practically inhaling a bottle of vodka. Does this normally occur when I am not home or are you just too stoned to notice?"

"Must you shout? I'm not deaf," Emma's eyes flapped up like shutters. Leaning into Gillian, she whispered in her ear. Smug, Gillian turned to walk away.

"I'm not done with you," James said.

Turning around, Gillian laughed, "You're pathetic." He only heard her feet skitter up the staircase and the slam of her bedroom door. Bunny sat there the whole time sucking his thumb.

"Welcome home, James." Emma waved her hand and walked to the counter, pausing over the pile of photos. Lifting one, then another, she dropped them to the floor. She sauntered out of the kitchen, her robe floating behind her like a train.

James said, "So this is a home."

Bunny picked up two Polaroids. With cactus arms, he held them high in the air. "Dad? Who are all these girls?", his ten-year-old son had asked. "And why are you kissing them?"

Bunny rubs his coat pocket and frowns. They all stand uncomfortable in front of the Canal Street train station, uneasy of sharing each other's air. Unzipping his coat, small porcelain cow and pig figurines tumble to the ground. Bunny moves in circles, gathering his stolen bounty. He cradles the knick-knacks in his hands. Two plastic Menudo dolls protrude from either side of Bunny's pant pockets. Gillian diverts her attention from James to her brother, twisting stands of her blond hair now streaked with chunks of periwinkle. "Bun, what did you do?" Gillian says, chewing on split ends.

James turns away from his children and descends into the station. The scent of Emma hangs deftly in the air around him. While he waits on line for tokens, James is almost convinced he will choke. Scanning the station, he prays for emergency exit routes, anything to escape his family. He hopes a train pulls into the station before his children make it to the platform. With one foot then the other, he would hop over the turnstile and sprint through the steel double doors. Leaving his children behind, he would wave to them through the windows of the car. James begins to give this fantasy serious thought. He would ride the subway all day—Brooklyn to the Bronx and back again. He would carve out a section of the train for himself, a two-seater, at the end of the car. With one foot propped up tapping the steel pole and the other dangling over the armrest, James would flick the pages of the *New York Post* loudly and read the paper cover to cover, including the ads. Licking his thumbs stained black with ink, he would turn each page. James would call this home.

"Dad, I need more." In his palm, Bunny reveals two quarters wet from his sweat.

"What he means, James, is that we need money for tokens," Gillian says and turns to her brother. "Don't worry, Bun."

"I'm not," he says.

"Then, Gillian, dear, pull out your wallet from under the coat that I bought you and buy them yourself. You can manage that, can't you? Or do you need to be hand-held in the process?" A train pulls into the station and the doors open and close within seconds, taking James's fantasy to the next stop.

"Right," Gillian replies, voice faltering. She turns her back to her father. A line begins to form in back of his daughter, snaking through the station. The booth collector smiles and nods and scratches his head with one hand and pulls the microphone to his lips with the other. His hoarse voice cuts in and out. He is giving directions.

"For Chrissake, Gillian." James yanks her from the line, and the three, with tokens in hand, move through the turnstiles and to the subway platform. Releasing his tight grip, Gillian stumbles back. For a moment, terror washes her face. James has never laid a hand on her. Wrapping her sweater around her arm, she bites down on her lip, hard. James begins to apologize,

"Gills," he says.

"Don't," she says. "Just don't."

The dead eel slides out of Bunny's coat onto the concrete. Pearl droplets of mucus secrete from its skin. At the middle of the platform, a child starts to wail. Not muffled, choked, sniffled cries, but a full-blown, mouth-stretched-wide, teeth-shaking, foot-stomping wail. The mother slaps the child in the back and, with the side of her sneaker, kicks the eel off the platform down into the track.

"I can't bring it home now," Bunny says. And then he laughs and looks up at James. "Everyone wants to leave us."

Drawing her brother close, Gillian holds him in her thin arms. "Bun, you okay?"

"Gillian, let go," he says. "I can't breathe." Bunny looses his grip on the figurines and they collapse to the ground, shattering into pink and white shards.

Looking down at Bunny, James asks, "What's going on?" Not that he ever knows. He wants to pat his son on the shoulder as fathers do pat their sons on their shoulders but he feels oddly repulsed by the whimpering child. All he wants to do is hand Bunny a Kleenex and run.

"Forget the Hard Rock," Bunny says. "I want to go home." Tears spill down his face. A mass of snot forms above his upper lip. James shudders. Where is Emma? She is always so good at these situations. She would have held Bunny to her breast. "It'll all be fine dear," she would coo and rub her nose against his. James wonders if he can learn to coo.

"Your son, James, your son stole a live fish from the market and shoved it in his jacket." Gillian pulls a Kent 100 from her coat pocket and strikes a match. Pointing to the dead fish, she says, "This isn't normal behavior for a twelve-year-old." The flame quickly burns down to the end of the match. An oval blister forms on Gillian's finger. "Fuck!" she shouts, shaking her finger.

What he has done to deserve this? James eyes his daughter's cigarette. "Put that out," he says through clenched teeth. A cluster of teenagers huddled in bulky coats turns and stares. Some snicker and point at them.

"Make me," she says.

"Keep your voice down, Gillian," he says. "Get yourself together, son." Leaning down, James quickly picks up the pieces of porcelain and shoves them in Bunny's pocket. "All better?"

"I can't hold on to anything," Bunny says. His tone abruptly shifts from hysteria to flat and controlled. Although he has stopped crying, Bunny's eyes are swollen and red. His cheeks puff like down pillows. James offers him a Dunkin Donuts napkin because he doesn't know what else he can do. Snatching the napkin, Gillian crouches down to wipe her brother's face clean, dabbing him softly as if he is china. An unlit cigarette dangles from the front of her mouth.

"Everything is breaking," Bunny says.

"You knew and did nothing?" James turns to Gillian. A train pulls into the station. James covers his ears as the screech of the brakes slamming the rails momentarily deafens him. He is tired of fighting with his defiant daughter who for the past two years knew of his indiscretions. Those damn pictures, he thought, upbraiding himself for buying her that camera. After that day two years ago, he took her on drives. He tried to explain how these things happen, how love can thin and fade. But Gillian had none of it. Folding her arms tight across her chest, she had said, "Is that it? Is that the best you can do?" He had rebuttals mapped out on cheat sheets—slips of colored paper. But Gillian had waved him away: "I'm done listening." The drives ended.

"Isn't that your job?" Gillian says, snapping James out of his thoughts. Puffing away, she continues, "But from what I heard, it won't be any longer." She steps through the opened double doors of the six train.

"I'm okay, Dad, really." Bunny raises his hand in defeat and follows Gillian into the train. Gillian extends her hand behind her and Bunny grabs it. A few curls dangle below his eyelid. He nibbles at his fingernails, chewing to the skin. Gillian makes eye contact with the male passengers in the subway car. She lifts the folds of her wool sweater to show a sliver of smooth, ripe skin. Some smile and nod until they see the father smack her hand down and zipper his daughter's coat. Suddenly, all gazes drop to the floor in a sudden floor fixation. Reaching in her bag, Gillian pulls out her Walkman and a Blondie cassette. She blasts "Rapture."

After seven subway stops, a perky waitress escorts James, Gillian, and Bunny through the mouse maze that is the Hard Rock Café. Her name, prominently displayed on her tag, reads "Bunny." She blows and crackles Bubble Yum, leading the three to their table. Her blond hair is woven into tight, long braids that rest on her breast. She is dressed in a black and white pinstripe shirt covered with buttons that read "We card your grandmother, SORRY!" and a thin, micro-mini black skirt. A Hard Rock Café cap is slung to one side. James licks his lips and rubs his chin with one hand, roving his fingers from one side of his face to the other.

"Can you be more obvious?" Gillian says, sliding into the corner of the tall, black leather booth. Bunny sits next to her, immediately immersed in the appetizer section of the menu. "She has my name," he whispers to no one.

"The waitress, that's my name."

"Just shut up, Gillian, and look at the menu," James snaps, flipping though the drink menu. He settles on a scotch.

"You're embarrassing me." Gillian stares at the plastic showcasing cheeseburgers and steaks. James ignores her. Bunny, the waitress, teeters over, pad in hand and says, "How would you like to hear our specials?"

"Dewar's, neat," James says.

"Gin and tonic," Gillian says. "Coke," James intercedes. Bunny, the waitress, nods and winks at James. James winks back.

"I'll have a Coke. My name is Bunny," Bunny says. His eyes widen as he stares at the waitress.

"Oh isn't that just the cutest!" she shrieks. For a moment, they all think that the waitress might pinch Bunny's cheeks.

"We're all just bouncing up and down with joy!" Gillian says. "Greek salad and fries."

"Bunny will have the hot dog and fries," James says and nods at his son. Bunny shrugs his shoulders.

"Fine. Whatever," Bunny says.

The waitress scribbles the orders down and smiles. "I'll be right back with your drinks!" James pictures the waitress with pom poms and a megaphone.

"Well," James says clapping his hands. He rubs them so hard that he could have started a fire.

"Well what?" Gillian says, "Is this the point where you play father?" She drums her long fingernails on the greasy table. James stumbles to fill the air with any form of conversation. Reaching within his coat to pull out the cards which all fall under the table, James bows his head under to reach for them but Gillian has scraped them to her side of the table with her feet.

"I know why we're here," she says. Bunny nods. "I know, James," she repeats.

Surprised and not armed with drink, James retreats further into the booth. Gillian slouches in her seat, her eyes menacing. He pictured pleas and all of the fanfare and confetti. Instead, his children have known all along and they hate him for it. Clutching his water glass, he grows angry. He wanted to explain this to his son rather than have Gillian taint the story. There would have been a chance that he would leave and his son would have understood.

"I don't know what your mother told you," James begins.

"She told us about her. About you and her." Gillian says, wringing the napkin in her hands.

"Dad, what is going to happen to us? We're not going to live with her, are we?" Bunny chokes on "her."

"Fat fucking chance, Bun. We are not going anywhere. I can't possibly understand, James, how you would think we would ever forgive you for this—much less live with you."

"Gillian, it isn't like that. Give me five minutes here!" Why had it been so easy to tell his wife? His teenage daughter gives him vertigo.

"I can't believe you're leaving me." Gillian rises from the booth. James frantically fans his hands down, motioning for her to sit.

"Nothing has changed. Me leaving changes nothing," James says.

"Keep telling that to yourself. Maybe one day, you'll believe it."

"Why is this happening to us?" Bunny asks. James and Gillian are immersed in their anger, ignoring Bunny. Bunny places his two small hands on the table and hoists his chest up onto the napkins and flatware that decorate the table and asks, "Dad, why?"

He remembers one of the phrases from the index cards and shouts, "We're still a family!"

Bunny falls back into his seat and shakes his head sadly. "No we're not."

"You got that right, Bun. How did you expect us to react? Did you think I would eat my fucking fries and just sit back and take it? How am I supposed to go to school on Monday? Did you think about that, James?" Tears slowly trickle down the side of her face. James falls silent. He has never seen his daughter cry.

"Gillian." James leans over the table and Gillian presses her shoulder blades into the leather booth.

"You don't deserve our love," Gillian says.

Bunny, the waitress, comes over with the drinks and food and pauses at the tense scene. Smiling nervously she says, "Let me know if you all need anything else." She sprints to the back of the restaurant. Gillian picks up one fry at a time and eats slowly. This is not how he had pictured this scene to go. This is all terribly, terribly wrong. After Gillian finishes her last fry James attempts again to explain the situation, to plead his case, but she has already closed her eyes. It's done.

"I'm still your father," he says.

"I'm angry that I allowed myself to love you," she says coldly. "Two years back—those drives. You acted so sincere. God was I a fucking idiot."

"You wouldn't listen! I tried to explain . . ."

"I don't understand. Make me understand, Dad." Gillian turns to her brother fidgeting in the booth. "Bunny, do you understand?"

"No," he says, "I don't."

Gillian rises and heads towards the bathroom. Face streaked with mascara and tears, his daughter is the image of Emma. All the women in his life turn their backs to him.

"So what are we going to do, Dad? What are we going to do?" Bunny pleads.

LAUREL

Heather Shaw

You're sitting on his porch and he wants you to leave but you can't leave, you don't want to and you can't. He's telling you that it's too cold but you're numb and you don't feel it and all you know is that he wants you to leave. He said he was breaking up with you and your mind started swimming then and it hasn't come up for air and you're drowning, drowning because you can't understand why he did that and why you have to leave. If you leave he's going to be gone forever, you'll lose your chance and he'll slip easily away and you need him, you need him. He's telling you to leave again, that you can talk about it tomorrow, but all you know is that if you leave then there is no tomorrow and you'd rather freeze here in the cold that you don't feel anyway. He asks you if he hits you will you leave and you're crying, "I don't know, I don't know," because at least then he'd be touching you, noticing you. But he doesn't hit you and you cry even harder because he doesn't care. So he fucked your best friend and she lied and he lied and you're saying this to him and all he says is Leave! Leave! You need to Leave! But you need him more and you're numb and you don't know what you look like sitting by his door and you don't know anything at all except you need him and you don't know how to keep him. He tells you you're cold and you tell him you don't feel it, all you feel is him. And he tells you he's cold and threatens to take off his shirt. And you're crying and he takes his shirt off and he's standing there all skinny and alone in front of his apartment and shivering. And you cry even harder because he's hurting himself to make you leave but you can't even do that for him because you can't stand the thought of losing him. And his body's turning white and cold and his freckles are standing out alone on his pale body and he looks so young and thin and you just want to reach out and hold him in your arms and you're crying harder and harder and your need to hold him is so much you can hardly stand it and you're begging him to put his shirt back on, to go inside and get a coat and he's getting angrier with you and telling you he will if you'd just Leave but you can't, you just can't and now he's mad and you're so scared, so scared because he might get mad enough to just go inside and forget about you and at least he's still out here telling you to leave. He's yelling now, probably because he's cold and tired and you're not leaving and you're trying to convince him you need him even though he made the mistake and now he knows he's so bad for you but you don't care, you don't care because you need him more than he can hurt you and you hope he hurts you. you hope he does something just as long as he's there, noticing you. He's putting his shirt back on and he's very angry because now he's giving in and walks over to you and he spits on you and he says, Look! I just spit on you! I spit on you, you should leave! You're going to let me spit on you? And you're wiping the spit off your face and crying because you don't care that he spit on you. And you feel like shit for sitting there next to his door, crying and wiping spit off your face at three in the morning and you can't believe he did that and you can't believe you're just sitting there after he spit on you and you feel like shit, you feel like nothing and you are nothing and you don't care, you don't care because you need him you need him you want to be nothing as long as you're with him. And you're crying and trying to tell him that you'll be anything anything and nothing as long as you're with him and he's shaking his head and you're hopeful, so hopeful you don't want to think about it because it would hurt too much if you fucked it up now by hoping too much but there's that look on his face and you wince because it's pure pity and it's pathetic and it's everything you've been hoping for all night because he's kneeling down beside you and saying, ok, ok, we're not breaking up. And he's putting his arm around you and pulling you into him and you're so happy so happy. You can't see now because your eyes are swollen and you're numb and you can feel how cold he is and now you're cold too, though you couldn't feel it before and now you can feel how tired he is. You are tired and you can see now what you look like slumped against the brick wall beside his door with your eyes swollen shut and the mascara running down your cheeks and you look horrible, you look terrible but you're happy, happy because he's pulling you up and leading you inside his apartment where it's warm and you can feel it now, covering you seeping inside you and you're with him and he's touching you and he's saying he's going to stay with you and you're happy and you're him and you're so happy and you're terrified he'll leave again because now you've got him and you could lose him and he could take you out of him and you would no longer be nothing because you wouldn't have him and you're scared so scared.

AFTER HOURS

Jonathan Harper

Out of all the coworkers, Claudia is the most outspoken about her affairs. Despite the lack of space, the break room is always full at noon, as the bookstore doesn't usually get busy until after three. All of the girls gather together around the small card table, drinking coffee and smoking cigarettes, while they gossip about the men that circulate in and out of their lives. Claudia's tales are the most impressive, not because she is particularly kinky in her sex, but because she sees a new man almost every week despite the fact that she has lived with her boyfriend for more than four years. Shortly after meeting her latest fling, she flaunts her disgust with her current relationship. But after the short-lived romance has ended, her boyfriend is suddenly a martyr, is sensitive to her needs, listens to her and always had a much larger penis. The other girls nod their heads in agreement and completely sympathize with her woes over men.

Paul, the assistant manager, usually scoffs lightly at Claudia's speeches, rolling his eyes at times with a half-smirk. He doesn't usually speak up unless spoken to, but is polite and sensitive to the needs of his employees. You like him, try to stand close to him; never too close, but close enough to refill his coffee before he moves for the pot.

"You always do that to me!" Claudia protests when he has made himself obvious. When she challenges him, the room erupts with staged gasps and chuckles. This i s when you usually back away from the two of them and linger in the far corner, rubbing elbows with the sink faucet. "Don't try and play so proud, either. We all know about you." Her eyes swell and light up as she looks back over the little congregated audience. You fear that she will eventually point at you.

But Paul never loses his composure. "So sorry to disappoint you. I guess I'm just boring."

Claudia's face relaxes. "I guess so," she replies with a sense of premature triumph. She wants to fuck him and everybody knows it.

Paul has been married to his wife for almost seven years and has a young son in the first grade. He is a gigantic man, well over six feet and pushing two hundred pounds. You've never seen him without his faded red baseball cap. You like him. He was the one who hired you, spoke softly during your training and made sure to include you in the staff's conversations. For him, you learned to enjoy the bitter taste of coffee, read all of his favorite books, and offered to stay late when needed.

The bookstore locks its doors every night religiously at nine. By this time, you have usually left and are either on your way home or out at one of the little cafés that litter the streets of Adams Morgan and Dupont Circle. But tonight, you are scheduled to close, which means watching most of the employees take off for their nightly destinations and cleaning the front area. Closing isn't difficult, it is just time consuming. You count the register drawer and then leave it in the office for Paul. Then, there are the arduous tasks of restocking the bookshelves, vacuuming the main areas, and cleaning up the break room. It is the break room that usually takes the longest, as the sink is always overloaded with chipped mugs, the counter tops are stained with dried coffee, and you seem to be the only employee capable of emptying the trash. Once you are finished, it is up to Paul to let you clock out before heading to the metro. Your boyfriend, Todd, sometimes picks you up afterward, but it is a Saturday and by this time he is usually at one of the bars, drinking his second or third gin and tonic.

This particular night, you finish earlier than expected. Paul has already shut himself up in the office, doing mundane paperwork or perhaps preparing to do inventory. It's not too late, you know you can punch out your time card, leave through the back door and rush out through the alley. But you still approach the office door, though your stomach swells with anxiety. You raise your hand once, twice and then finally tap your fingers against the wood. Perhaps it will go unnoticed or Paul will ignore it tonight because of his workload. There is a sigh of relief when it seems your knocking will go unanswered and you turn to leave.

But the door opens behind you. "Come in," he says with a very straight face. There is no emotion behind this. He apparently does not share your anxiety; he does not notice your hands quivering. But you walk in past him and retreat to the side wall next to the file cabinets. Paul just reseats himself behind the desk. "One of the drawers came up short today," he says with a stern voice.

"Which one?"

"Not yours, don't worry about it." This means it's either Claudia or the new girl. Claudia is the girl you dread to stand next to for too long. She likes her gossip and tends to probe others a little too deeply. Still, you would hate to think that she is coming one step closer to being fired. "You locked up front, right? Because you forgot the other night. You're lucky I checked before I left."

This is how it begins, you think.

Paul finishes recording the drawer amounts and places the money in the safe. "You should know better by now," he reminds you sternly as he beckons. You come willingly; you have gone this far before and know what to expect. He remains seated, seems to admire the thickening of your groin. He is on you in moments, a hand around your waist as he brings his other against your backside.

Every slap is for your father. This is the punishment you never received but always deserved for every ill thought, every fantasy that you masturbated to in the quiet of your childhood bedroom.

Paul slides down your pants so you are fully exposed. The air conditioner gives your ass goose bumps. He says you're fattening up just nice, pokes and prods you. This is for your mother, who bound you with wicked words and insults. She was the one who said she loved you the most and prayed for your sins in front of the entire family. She inspected you for faults, made you feel naked while clothed and made you bleed without any cutting. Though your knees shake, though you fear being caught half-naked under Paul's weight, you do not try to conceal your crotch or reach for your pants.

Paul unzips, spits and fucks you hard. As one small act of defiance, you rock your hips back to match his movements. You smile to yourself secretly, let his hands grasp your arms so tightly that you almost bruise. This is for your brothers, the ones who would have left you for dead if they could, who knocked you down, ordered you about, and demanded to be thanked for making you tough. And you are thankful, just in a way they would never expect.

Somewhere along the way, Paul comes and then withdraws from you before collapsing back into the chair. You are still leaning forward, a little unsatisfied. It's never as exciting as the first time. When you turn, he is rubbing himself with the little rag he keeps in his backpack. It's the only time you get to see his cock, softened and exhausted. His smile reeks of personal gratification. It is both malevolent and endearing at the same time. You stare back sullenly, leave your pants undone, and make your way out to the restroom.

This is the last part of your evening, behind the locked door of the unisex restroom. You try to relive every moment of the experience. You masturbate hard, almost breaking your own skin with the dry strokes. This is for Todd, the one who promised to keep you safe, the one who holds you gently, and the one who doesn't believe in just fucking. You think of him and his silly habits: The way he likes to juggle his keys before leaving for work, the way he bites the skin around his finger nails, or the ridiculous exercise routine he does every morning. You imagine Todd is suddenly behind you, holding you by the hair, fucking you harder than before, spitting out venom and curses. You can almost feel it like little tremors, his face suddenly older, twisted but beautiful and his lips curling into a snarl. It is then that you finally get off, almost gasping for air—you had held your breath until the end. Then you clean yourself off, clock out and walk out through the alley and to the metro.

Your boyfriend, Todd, is closer to your height, but, like Paul, is almost a decade older than you. He is trim and handsome, has a law degree, and makes decent money on Capitol Hill. The two of you share an apartment near the Cleveland Park metro station. It is well furnished; most of the décor is out of your price range. With the exception of the bookcases and the volumes of mix-matched literature, nothing belongs to you. The guest bedroom features your neglected writing desk and the futon that was your bed throughout college. Your mother doesn't approve and has never asked to come over. She calls once every other week and tells you about your older brother's house in New Jersey. "Like a mansion," she insists. "Maybe you can find a real job and a nice girl to settle down with." Todd is understanding after you've suffered through these conversations. He makes living here seem all too secure and comfortable. It is always clean, unlike your mother's cluttered kitchen. The smell of beer and sounds of football games never echo from the living room. You are relatively bruise-free from the absence of your older brothers.

You make love with Todd only once or twice a week, which is far less than you used to. You blame it on your work schedule or the occasional late nights out with your remaining college friends. He purchases ginseng pills for you, thinking they will help. He always kisses you passionately, pulls your hips towards his own, enters you slowly, and fucks in short gentle rhythms. But there are still things he cannot do for you. You push against him with force, release the bottled-up aggression and he soothes you to a small climax. The entire effort is exhausting. There is usually no smoking allowed in bed, just one last kiss and then the weight of his body that presses down firmly against the mattress.

You don't go out to the bars often. When you do, it is usually alone while Todd is out of town on business. The men there are twice your age and treat you like a commodity. They buy your drinks and talk to you with slurred speech. Every so often, you let them slip a few fingers into your pockets or let them grind their waist against the back of your pants. It never goes any further, as you disappear into the crowd before these admirers can invite you back to their homes. You are sure, one night, you see Paul standing in the corner and sipping a beer. He has probably told his wife that he is out with his friends for the evening or is at the bookstore doing inventory. You are tempted to walk up and speak to him, to talk to him like it's another casual afternoon in the break room. However, he leaves before you can muster up the courage.

On the occasional Saturday morning, Todd drives you in to work and Paul usually invites him into the break room for a morning cup of coffee and a doughnut. This is nerve-racking, seeing the both of them together. Your stomach always squirms, wondering if the conversation will ever turn away from the polite small talk. Thankfully, it never lasts for long. Claudia usually interrupts, gloating over her latest exploits to Todd before he excuses himself and leaves for home. Paul never acknowledges the shamed looks you give him, though you don't disguise your guilt.

The next time you close with Paul, he follows you into the bathroom and fucks you hard in front of the small mirror. Your hands brace themselves against the sink and you accidentally knock over the small ceramic soap dispenser, which shatters. You start to loose your concentration, staring at the pieces. Your erection suffers, but Paul does not notice. You stare up at him in the mirror, realizing it is the first time you've seen his face while he fucks you, precise and mechanical.

The store closes early on Halloween because many people are taking their children out for trick-or-treating or will be throwing costume parties. Your mother calls that evening, asking about your plans for Thanksgiving. She makes a point not to invite Todd. You inform her that you'll have to leave early that weekend to be at work by Saturday and she berates you for not staying to go to church with the family. She mentions that all your brothers have taken the whole weekend off and you remind her that they work normal business hours. Her response is to tell you to find a better job until you finally hang up on her. Todd suggests you fly out to Seattle with him to visit his parents. You politely decline and tell him to go without you, which upsets him. You may feel guilty, but rationalize that you really do need the time alone.

You are not scheduled to close with Paul for quite some time. At first this is a relief, but you find yourself frustrated when you leave at night. You think about lingering some nights or switching shifts, but then think better of it. You and Todd make love more often. You crawl all over him, guide his hands to the right places, but it isn't the same. Todd tells you later that he thinks the ginseng pills are helping and you simply release a heavy sigh.

You start to wonder if Paul has grown tired of you. You and he don't talk much in the break room. He seems more distant than usual. You bluntly offer to close a few nights the following week.

"I can't just change the schedule like that. If you want to close, switch with someone," he says. You nod with disappointment and silently pray that he notices.

In the break room, Claudia tells you about a new man who wanted to handcuff her to his bed and piss on her. She laughs and says, "He's completely insane! I mean, who in their right mind would ever go through with that? I told him to fuck off right then and there and then told him to find some other bitch and now he's been calling my cell phone and leaving these creepy messages."

You chuckle lightly. "Where do you find these people?"

"Online, of course. I mean, I wasn't planning on doing him or anything. We just met up for drinks and then ended up back at his place." Her voice is playful and she wants you to question her.

"It sounds like you knew what he wanted."

She gives you a smirk and lights a cigarette. "Yeah, I knew. I just didn't think it would involve any pissing." She exhales out smoke that spirals through the long strands of her red hair. "Men are like that. They let you think one thing and then expect another. You know how it is."

Paul has entered during this and begins to refill his coffee. You meet his gaze and then he abruptly walks out. "Not really," you struggle to say just in time for him to hear.

Claudia watches this with great intensity. Her voice is reduced to a small whisper. "Of course you do. And everyone knows it." Her eyes narrow a little as she takes another drag. "You know, the only difference between you and I is that I don't try to hide it."

Later, Claudia asks you to close for her. At first, you refuse, explaining that you have dinner plans with Todd, but she calls your bluff and begs. You reluctantly agree and Claudia smiles mischievously and runs into the office to tell Paul. You call Todd and tell him you'll be home late and he groans over the phone.

You lock the door at nine and glare at Claudia as she winks at you on her way out. You deposit your drawer in the office as early as possible and rush through the cleaning. Tonight your stomach feels sour and you develop a headache. You do not linger in the break room for a cigarette and you toss out the coffee early on. You do however, linger outside the door to the office, wanting just to shout through the door that you are leaving.

But it's the sudden knocking at the front door that attracts your attention. Paul emerges from his chambers and looks at you puzzled.

"Don't they realize we're fucking closed," he mumbles as he walks out to the front door.

Todd is waiting outside and Paul lets him in, smiling politely. "I figured since you had to work late, I'd just pick you up myself," Todd says while hugging you warmly.

You thank him, eager to leave. But Paul offers him a cup of coffee and walks back to the break room. The three of you sit around the small card table, Paul and Todd both sipping from mugs of decaf. You are silent and listening to them bullshit about the latest movie releases. Paul is polite and social but does not include you in the conversation. At one point, Todd suggests that you and he try to catch up with some friends out at the bar and you suddenly realize that you've been staring at Paul for most of the conversation. You can barely stay focused enough to nod yes.

There is something small and remarkable about this moment. This is the first time you've witnessed a real conversation between Paul and Todd. It should seem ordinary and irrelevant. You will later go out to a small bar with Todd and drink so much that he will have to practically carry you back to the car. You will go home and he will hold you in bed so tightly that you'll almost vomit under his weight. Paul will go home to his wife and kiss her lightly before eating the leftover dinner she kept warm for him. For this one moment, you can forget what Claudia told you that morning, forget about the possible events that could have taken place behind the office door. You sit there, watching them together and sizing them up for what they're worth. There are things one can do that the other can't. And this is the moment when you suddenly realize that as much as you want them both, you really don't want either at all.

ALL THE BAD STUFF

Barry Graham

for Dennis Cooper

I waited outside the theater, but they didn't show up. I was a few minutes late, but I'd have expected Andy to wait for me. It would be at least another thirty minutes before the movie started. Maybe Leanne had gotten impatient and dragged him inside.

I bought a ticket and went in. It was already pretty busy, mostly kids with their parents, but also the odd adult sad case sitting alone. There was no sign of Andy and Leanne. I went outside, found a phone and called him. His machine came on. He always screened his calls. "Hey, this is Andy. I'm not here right now, but then neither are you. If you were, maybe I would be too." Bleep.

"Hi, it's Ken. You're not here, either. Are you home? No? Okay, maybe you're on your way. I'll see you."

I went back inside. The trailers were showing. I sat down and spread my jacket across the two seats next to mine, claiming them for Andy and Leanne.

The place filled up. A few minutes before the movie started, a woman nudged me. "Excuse me. Are those seats taken?" She had a girl of about ten with her.

"Kind of. Not really." I lifted my jacket from the seats. She sat down on the seat beside mine, the kid sitting on the other side of her. "I'm waiting for a couple of people," I told her. "But it doesn't look like they're coming. You'll have to give them the seats if they do show."

"Yeah, no problem." She was in her mid-twenties, with long, dark hair and what I recognized as a Jim Rose Sideshow T-shirt in the light from the screen.

The movie was just about to start. "Okay, you've got the seats," I said. "I'm going."

"Since you've paid, you should stay and watch the movie."

I laughed. The movie was *The Lion King*. "You need to have a kid with you to get into a movie like this. I was supposed to meet a friend and his daughter."

"Well, I've brought a kid. You can share."

I was surprised. I'm not the Elephant Man, but I'm not Brad Pitt either. Women usually only go for me after we've talked a lot and I've managed to convince them that looks aren't important. And this one was cute.

"Okay," I said.

The movie wasn't bad. Totally fascist message, of course, but with some okay songs and animation. I didn't follow the story too well—I just sat there and tried to believe my good luck. Or what seemed like good luck. Could I be getting it wrong? Maybe it didn't mean she was into me. Maybe she was just weirdly friendly. Maybe she was just weird. Throughout the movie, she looked at me periodically and smiled and shared her bag of M&Ms with me. That seemed promising.

When the movie ended, we went outside into the lobby. I looked at her. In the darkness, her hair had just looked dark. Now I saw that it was a shiny black. And she looked amazing. I wondered if she was looking at me and deciding that what was intriguingly grotesque in a darkened theater was actually pretty gruesome in daylight.

We just stood there, smiling. The kid stared at us, not smiling. "What're you doing now?" I asked.

"I have to get Caroline home. Are you doing anything tonight?"

"I have to work."

"What is it you do?"

"I'm kind of in movies." I grinned at her. "I work in a video store."

She laughed and asked which one. I told her. "Maybe I'll call you there," she said.

"Great. Or call me at home." I wrote my name and phone number on the back of my ticket to the movie. She got out her own ticket, wrote on it and handed it to me. I looked at it. Her name was Shari.

The video store wasn't artsy. It was in the scummy part of town, where I lived, and the stock—action, porno, and splatter—reflected the discerning tastes of our clientele.

I was quite a star to our customers, or at least to the more sociopathic among them. I know just about everything there is to know about splatter movies, especially low-budget, straight-to-video-with-no-theatrical-release ones. I'm also pretty good on obscure foreign stuff, particularly Japanese splatterpunk. My expertise was held in such high regard by the local thugs that many of them no longer chose their own movies, but asked me instead. It was a dangerous neighborhood, but I was under the protection of the gang that controlled it. They loved me because I'd recommended the Japanese classic *Tetsuo II: The Body Hammer*. Their leader was so impressed by it that he changed his name from Drillboy to Tetsuo.

I started playing up to my celebrity. I'd go to work dressed entirely in black, with either a skull or an upside-down crucifix dangling from my ear. Everyone who worked in the store had to wear a badge with their name on it. The boss let me change my name to suit my persona. My badge had originally said Ken. Now it read The Prince of Darkness.

On that Saturday night, I worked from five until midnight. Towards closing time, I was debating whether to head downtown to a club or go home and watch *Stuff Stephanie in the Incinerator*, which I'd finally managed to get a copy of after a long search.

Then Shari came in. "Hi," she said, like there was nothing unusual about her being there.

"Hi."

She was wearing a leather jacket and tight black jeans. A watch cap with a baseball logo clung to her head, her long hair spilling from under it. She looked at my apparel. "I didn't realize you were a goth."

"I'm not. It's part of my job to look like this. I run the horror section."

"I like scary movies."

"What brings you down here?"

She smiled, embarrassed. "Instead of calling you, I thought I'd come by and say hello. So hello."

I smiled back at her, trying to think of something to say.

"Did you find out what happened to your friend?" she asked me.

"Yeah. After he picked up his daughter from his ex-wife, his car blew a gasket. Speaking of daughters, is the girl you were with today yours?"

"Caroline? No. I'm her honorary big sister. I do volunteer work at this organization that matches you with a troubled kid to hang out with."

"What do you do for involuntary work?"

She laughed. "I'm a dog groomer."

"What's that?"

"A person who grooms dogs."

"Yeah, no shit. I mean where do you get a job like that?"

"I work at the animal hospital. People bring in their mangy woof-woofs, and it's my job to tidy them up and hope they don't tear my throat out while I'm doing it."

"Do you like it?"

"Yeah, it's okay. It's a good no-brainer. I just go into robot mode and daydream."

"Listen, I get out of here at around midnight. Want to go do something?"

"Sure. What?"

"We could go to a club. Or, if you want to watch a movie, I live near here . . ."

"Okay."

Then I got flustered and started to babble. "Oh, and that isn't a line. I'm not coming on to you . . . Or rather, I am, but only if you want me to. If you don't, you can still come and watch a movie with me . . ."

"Okay." She was grinning.

"Do you have roommates?" she asked as we walked to my apartment.

"No. I live by myself. That's why I chose this part of town— rent's cheap. I can just about afford a place to myself. If I lived any-where else, I'd have to share."

It was a cold night. In my living room we could see our breath. I lit the gas heater. "My ears are frozen," said Shari. I clapped my hands together to warm them, then put a hand over each of her ears. We looked at each other's faces. She smiled. Never all that quick on the uptake, even I got the message. We kissed. Then we knelt on the floor in front of the heater and kissed some more. She'd taken off her jacket but was still wearing her cap. As we kissed, I pulled the cap off and stroked her hair.

We never saw the movie.

I don't like to rush into things—I believe you should know someone for at least a week before you move in together. That's how long it took for Shari to quit her apartment and move into mine.

Two days after our first meeting, I had to take a day trip to another town, to visit a friend who had just found out that he had cancer. I asked him whether a cure was likely. He said that the chances were remote and that he was trying to accept that he was going to die. I knew no way to comfort him.

On the bus home, I felt scared for him and for myself. I was also worried about how I was going to eat the following week. I'd had just about enough money to get through until the next paycheck, but the cost of the bus ticket had wiped out nearly half of it.

As the bus passed a long stretch of coastline, for the first time I took no pleasure in the sight of it. The water was almost still and the sun seemed to be sinking into it. But this time the beauty wasn't enough. Usually just a glimpse of it could instantly put me in a good mood, but now I realized—I'd always known, but never realized— that you can't escape to the sea. This isn't Han Shan's China or Thoreau's America. That's all gone now. If you decided you'd had enough and went off to live by the sea or up a mountain, you still couldn't get away from the need for money. They've made it so that money and sustenance are the same fucking thing.

When the bus arrived in town, I got off and decided to walk home. It was cold, but I was fretting too much to be able to stand still at a bus stop. I didn't have a car, and I couldn't afford a cab.

On the way home I ran into Franny. He saw me before I saw him, or else I'd have tried to avoid him. We used to play in a band together, and after that we washed dishes together in a restaurant kitchen, but I couldn't deal with him anymore. He'd always been erratic, but these days it seemed as though the alcohol that he practically lived on had driven him mad.

He was standing near a public phone, waiting to use it. "Ken!" he yelled, spiderlike in his huge black coat, eyes bugging out of his skeletal face.

"Hi, Franny."

"Where you going, man?"

"Home."

"Where you been?"

"Visiting this friend of mine. He's got cancer."

Franny shook his head, laughed, his long hair flailing. "Fuck cancer. Fuck everything."

As easy as that. How simple the world of the booze casualty.

I was suddenly close to tears. "No, Franny. Fuck you." I walked away from him. When I looked back he was laughing, giving me a clenched-fist salute, a we-know-the-score-pal salute. I flipped him the finger and kept walking.

I stopped at a deli and got some bread, pasta, and pesto sauce. When I got home I found Shari sitting cross-legged on the sidewalk outside the door of my apartment. She was reading a book, and she didn't see me until I kicked one of her feet.

She looked up, smiled hugely. "Hi!"

"Hi. How long've you been sitting there?"

"About twenty minutes. I was going to wait another ten, then give up and go."

"You should be careful. It's rough around here."

"Nobody hassled me." She stood up. "One dude thought I was begging. Gave me some change."

I unlocked the door and we went into the apartment. "You should have told me you were coming over. I'd have given you keys."

"I wasn't planning to. I just had a sudden notion to see you."

I put my arms around her. Warm smell of dog fur and shampoo.

"How was your friend?" she asked me.

I told her. She didn't say anything stupid, any of the things people normally say in that kind of situation. She didn't say anything. She just listened.

I cooked some pasta. We ate it and went to bed. Before I fell asleep, she pressed her mouth to my forehead. "I'm going to kiss you, and when I do all the bad stuff's going to go out of your head." She kissed me, and it mostly worked.

Sometime during the night I woke to find her stroking my hard cock. "Too tired," I mumbled.

"I know. But you don't have to do anything." She stroked me until I came all over us both. Then she held me tight and told me to go back to sleep and I did.

In the morning she had to go and groom some dogs. I didn't have to work until the afternoon. She got up at seven-thirty, made two mugs of coffee, and came back to bed.

"Do you want some breakfast?" I asked her as she handed me a mug.

"Nah. I have to rehydrate first. I'll get something on the way to work."

"This is going to sound stupid, coming after I've known you for four days. But I think I love you."

She looked at me for a second, then laughed and took a big slurp of coffee. "Yeah, that sounds pretty dumb. Not as dumb as me, though—I know I love you."

She moved in the next day. She'd been sharing a place, and we wanted to live on our own. Rather than look for someplace central—which would be expensive and a hassle—we decided to live in my happy hovel in the heart of slumland.

Our friends thought it was weird, us doing it so soon. But I never had any doubts. I once had a pretty intense relationship that lasted two years, during which I never once considered the possibility of us living together. After a few days with Shari, the idea of us not living together seemed weird.

I didn't have to get used to it. There wasn't any sense of novelty, of something new. It seemed natural, as though it had always been that way. I told her so, and she said it was the same for her.

Only one thing was strange: Suddenly we had two of just about everything—TV, VCR, stereo, etc. Hers and mine. We decided to mark our cohabitation by getting something that had never belonged to either of us alone, something that was entirely ours. I would have said that applied to most of my shirts, jackets and sweaters, which Shari now wore more often than her own stuff, but she was adamant about the necessity of ritual. We had to get something that had no history.

We got a wrought-iron candleholder. It had a gothic design and held two candles. We both liked it. I said we couldn't ever break up, because we'd both want the candleholder and you can't saw wrought iron in half.

I often talked on the phone with Colin, whose cancer was now beyond treatment. He said he'd realized that nothing that had ever happened to him really mattered. Everything now seemed to him to be at the same time laughably trivial and intensely important.

"Are you scared?" I asked him.

"Kind of. I'm not scared of what'll happen to me after I die, like if there's an afterlife or whatever. I don't even care that much about what happens to me then. I just don't want to go. I want to stay here. I don't want to leave the bands and the books and the movies I like, and I don't want to leave my friends. God . . ." He laughed miserably. "I'm talking like I'm only moving to another town or something. Listen, man, I'm getting maudlin. I'm gonna go, okay?"

"You can get maudlin if you want."

"Thanks, but I'd rather not. Come and see me soon, okay?"

"Yeah, of course. I'd come more often, but I haven't got the money for the bus. But I'll come next week sometime."

"Have you seen Neil?"

"Not in a while."

"If you see him, tell him to come and see me. He hasn't been in touch since I got really bad."

"I will."

The truth was that I had run across Neil once or twice, but I wasn't going to tell Colin. Neil was an old friend of his from college. He was an actor and wasn't getting the sort of work he wanted. He'd told me that he couldn't face going to see Colin because he was depressed about not getting work that was creatively fulfilling, and seeing Colin would depress him even further.

One memory of Colin that I took refuge in while he was dying: A few years earlier, we went to France together and ended up in Cannes during the film festival. We didn't have much money, so we didn't see many movies. We just hung out in the sun, in that weird wonderland atmosphere a place always has if it's summer and there's a festival going on. We drank and talked about maybe making a splatter movie on Super-8.

We shared a cheap room, where we went only to sleep. Colin had brought his guitar with him, so we did some busking. He was a good guitar player, I was pretty bad. Neither of us could sing, not that we let it stop us. I had brought along a Walkman and some tapes, including *Rock Animals* by Shonen Knife, my all-time favorite band. Colin wasn't keen on them, but he figured out the guitar parts on a few of their songs and tried to teach me to play them. I managed to learn "Music Square," a song Colin hated. I thought it was the most beautiful thing I'd ever heard. Colin said it was like the Carpenters with Japanese accents.

Colin got laid. I didn't. He always found it easier than I did. He was a handsome guy, and when he got some sun he looked like a Californian surfer. I was, and remain, a geek. But it wasn't geek-iness that kept me from getting laid. It was that I didn't want to. It was enough just to be there. It wasn't a lack of interest in the women I saw and sometimes talked to in cafes—but it was enough just to see them. Fucking wouldn't have added anything.

One evening I was out busking on my own. Colin was with a woman somewhere. I was sitting on a low wall near the sea. As I clumsily played "Music Square," a woman walked past. She had tangled brown hair and wore a white tank top with a long skirt. She looked at me. I smiled at her. She smiled back. She was painful-ly lovely. She hesitated. Then, when I didn't stop playing and talk to her, she continued walking.

I went on singing:
"I am very happy tonight
I could see the beautiful stars
I've been waiting for a long time
To come on Music Square."

The woman. White cotton against brown skin. Hair falling over it. Her smile before she walked away. Lovely young essence of her. The jangling of the guitar.

The way Colin ate tortilla chips. The veins on the backs of his hands.

Late at night. Shari cuddled close to me. Kissing all the bad stuff out of my head. All that she's made of, that I'm made of—

blood, bowels, heart, lungs, liver, kidneys, brain, bladder, pancreas. Nothing perfect or eternal.

Hey, death. Hey, death. Fuck you.

There was a woman who came into the video store a lot. We used to banter, though we didn't have much to talk about movie-wise. What can you say to a person whose favorite movie is *Field of Dreams*? I got the impression that she was into me, but even if I was single, I wouldn't have been interested. She looked like Tom Hanks.

Then, one night, I started coming on to her. I didn't know why I was doing it. She invited me to come to her place when the store closed. I said I couldn't, that my girlfriend would be expecting me home. She told me to come over the next morning if I wanted. She said she didn't care that I had a girlfriend. She didn't seem callous or nasty, just lonely and desperate.

I went to her place as soon as Shari had left for work. It was so sad; at eight-thirty in the morning she answered my knock wearing make-up, short skirt, black tights. So desperate to impress.

It was surprisingly good, right until I came. I came in her mouth, sitting on her couch with her kneeling on the floor between my legs. She tried so hard, stopping to recite, "Yeah, do it for me, give it to me." Then put my cock back in her mouth.

As soon as I came, everything changed. I was so sick with guilt I could have converted to Catholicism. I got dressed, saying I had to go. She asked when she'd see me again. I said I'd be in touch. She smiled tightly, letting me off easy.

All day I walked around like fucking Raskolnikov. I was supposed to work in the afternoon, but I called and got someone to swap shifts with me.

I wasn't going to tell Shari, but I had no choice. She knew something was wrong with me, and she knew I was lying when I said I was all right. It began to frighten her.

"Whatever's going on, I want you to tell me. Is it me? Have I done something wrong?"

When she said that, I couldn't not tell her. At first she thought I was joking, that I couldn't really have done it. When she realized that it wasn't a joke, she cried for a long time. I kept saying I was sorry. When she'd stopped crying she asked me, "Do you want to be with her?"

"No. I don't even know her."

"Why did you do it, then?"

"I don't know."

"Don't be stupid. Or treat me like I'm stupid. You must know."

"I don't. I can make something up if you want, but the truth is I don't know. I'm not even attracted to her looks."

She started to cry again, but anger choked it back. When she spoke I could hear the rawness in her throat. "Okay. You fuck around on me and you don't even know why. Great." She gestured towards the door. "Get out of here. Leave me alone for a while."

I told her again that I was sorry. Then I got my jacket and left. I went and saw a movie, then went to a diner and ate. It was only about nine o'clock, and I was too ashamed to go home and face Shari again. I sat in the place for another two hours, then walked home slowly, hoping she'd be asleep by the time I got there.

She'd gone. So had most of her stuff. The candleholder was gone too. There was a note, just the phone number I could reach her at.

I called it. The woman who answered had obviously heard the story. She wasn't friendly. "Just a minute," she barked when I asked to speak to Shari. I heard her call, "Shari—it's him."

"Hi," said Shari.

"Where are you?"

"At Ali's. You met her once."

"Oh, yeah."

"I'm staying with her till I find a place. I couldn't keep living with you."

"You didn't have to move out. You can have this place if you want it. I'll move out."

"No. It's your place. I'll find somewhere."

"I thought of it as our place."

"The only thing that was ours is the candleholder."

"I noticed you took that."

"Yeah. I think I'm entitled."

"I suppose so. Like I said, you can't saw wrought iron in half. I'll miss it, though."

"Will you miss me?"

"I love you."

"You've got a funny way of showing it."

"Shari, I'm so sorry."

"I'm going to hang up. I don't want to start crying again. It makes Ali feel bad."

I'd lived with Shari for eight months. Prior to that, I'd lived without her for almost thirty years. But with her gone, things didn't seem normal. I didn't fall apart; I went to work, and I dragged myself out to meet friends. But I couldn't make any plans or even think about what to do next. There was a feeling of things not being in their proper place, as though the order had been somehow disrupted. I felt like I was living in a state of flux, and though I told myself that it was permanent and I had to get on with it, it didn't seem like anything I would get used to.

Colin got worse. He became too weak to even talk on the phone for very long. He was in constant pain, and was only kept from agony by heavy doses of liquid morphine. He didn't want to die in a hospital, so he'd moved into his mother's house.

I have no religion, but I started praying. I didn't know who or what I was praying to. I didn't give it a name. I just knelt and clasped my hands and thought about Colin and tried to do him some good.

I got on a bus and went to visit him, knowing it would probably be the last time I'd see him. It would be a few weeks before I'd be able to afford the bus fare again, and his mother had told me he wasn't likely to live that long.

It was late afternoon when I got there. A hot day. I was wearing surfing shorts, a Butthole Surfers T-shirt and a Mickey Mouse baseball cap, which didn't strike me as being inappropriate until just before I arrived.

His mother let me in. She'd never liked me much. Colin had told me that she thought most of his friends were weird, especially me. It didn't seem to occur to her that he was in the company of his peers.

Poor woman. These days, she seemed glad to see me. She sat me down in her kitchen and told me, "Colin's asleep. Let's have some tea and see if he wakes up." She made the tea and asked about my life. I told her everything was fine, that Shari and I were okay. I kept it ambivalent; I didn't want to dump on her by telling the truth, and I was afraid to come on like Mr. Happy in case that made her feel worse.

She went upstairs to check on Colin. "He's still asleep," she told me when she came back. "I don't really want to wake him, Ken. He was in awful pain—he was crying from it. So he took a lot of morphine." She paused, thinking the same thing as me, that I wouldn't get to say goodbye to him face-to-face. "He'd want to see you, though. Do you want me to wake him?"

"No. I'll phone him. But is it okay if I just go in and see him? I won't wake him. I'll be really quiet."

She nodded, not liking it.

He looked dead, but he wasn't. His breathing was heavy. All that pain. Crying from it. I stood by his bed, looking down at him. Cannes. Shonen Knife. Neon rain. Late-night movies, years of them. Tortilla chips. His tan. His veins. His guitar. Beer. Tea. Liquid morphine.

I bent over him and whispered, so quietly he couldn't have heard it even if he'd been awake, "I'm going to kiss you, and when I do all the bad stuff's going to go out of your head."

His forehead was warm and dry against my lips. I stood and looked at him for a while, then left.

A couple of days later, Shari showed up at my apartment. "I brought you something," she said, as I let her in. She was carrying a big canvas bag.

We sat in the living room. She opened the bag and brought out the candleholder. "Here."

"But it's yours. You're entitled to it after what happened. You said so yourself."

She smiled nervously. "Yeah, but I know you really like it. So I brought it for you." She held it out to me.

Something about her doing that tore me open. I clenched my teeth and tried to swallow it down, but I couldn't. I cried, covering my face with my hands, almost roaring. Shari came over and put her arms around me, holding me, rocking me against her. She

CUCK(H)OLDING A STRANGER

Lenelle Moïse

It is Friday night and I am not with a boy I love. I'm not sure I can love a boy who calls me exotic; who tells me he is curious about people like me: people who smell black and have hair that can knot that smells black also; people whose thick rubbery-looking lips (brownish, gray) are actually soft and taste black also. I cannot love a white boy who mumbles along to the hip-hop lyrics crashing into his earphones as if they are gyrating towards his pelvis. He relates to me as if I am hip-hop also: Where there is certain hot revolt, he perceives casual, trendy cool.

I am not sure he would have asked me out last year if I had not been passing for middle class; if I, too, had not read *Catcher in the Rye* and *The* (stupid) *Great Gatsby* in our English seminar for "advanced" high school seniors. In class, if I had flinched when challenging his cockily delivered commentary instead of tearing his weak analysis apart, he would never have learned my name. My name is Rachel, pronounced the elegant French way because I have working-class Haitian roots. And though I resent this boy, I will defend him because he makes my stomach twist with certain lust and he tells me he wants me.

"He's Jewish," I told my bark-hued, seemingly militant uncle who visited me last week. My uncle is only three years older than I am, so we are friends. He is my height and attractive, so sometimes we put our arms around each other like lovers would in the street. Arms are the extent of it, but I adore him. He is a self-described strong black man with long bleached dreadlocks. He wears cowrie shells around his thick, shiny neck and sporty cloth-bracelets colored red, black, and green. When he played college football, he enjoyed tackling Caucasians "just because."

Last week, my uncle absolutely twitched when I showed him a photo of the white boy I do not love. "Jewish boys are different," I argued. I meant that my nineteen year-old heart senses a connection between the Holocaust and Jim Crow; my loins pulse with the notion that there is something integrated about jazz and jazz is my favorite kind of music. My uncle, however (who has flaunted various naturally blonde girlfriends in his lifetime, but claimed it was a sideshow), listens to reggae exclusively, and could give a shit about jazz. He shrugged at my idealism; he shouted, "A white boy won't never treat you right." My uncle cut his visit short, but before he left he warned, "Y'all better not be having sex."

It is Friday night and I am not having sex with a boy I love. We are not even holding hands. We are innocently on our way to a famous poetry café in the lower east section of an island called the City. There will be two featured performers, a poetry slam, an after hours open mic. I will recite in the latter; I will recite about jazz. He is there to support me is all, as a friend, the white boy. He isn't my current boyfriend, really, just someone I want to feel close to; who knows why? He has olive skin—dark, nappy hair—shouldn't we feel closer? Isn't it important to feel close to a boy who, just three months ago in his warm college dorm room, sweetly manipulated my moans?

I was a virgin then, and astonished. He was determined, brave, intense. He used soft palms to press against my orange tights, which, despite his giddy pleading, I would not let his teeth pull off. I told him I was holding out for the Lord and I meant it but we laughed, long.

Then, out of order—clothed beneath him clothed—I pulled his head into my first kiss. So maybe we'd marry someday. He could be my benefactor; I could be an eating actress. His fore-parents were slave captors; my body near him could ease his guilt. Besides, I was his favorite high school sweetheart and wouldn't it be romantic?

It is Friday night—and cold—and I'm with a boy who barely knows me. He doesn't know I no longer consider myself a virgin, because I penetrate myself. He doesn't know I've decided the Lord I once held out for isn't in the sky, or a man, or anywhere else—anyone else—I am not. He doesn't realize I am using him; walking beside him to feel like a simple, skirted, normal girl; he doesn't know I sometimes think of his sister when, all alone, I touch my skin even when it is his name that pants out of my mouth. His name is

Noah, pronounced the way people always pronounce it here because, until the High Holidays, he pretends his people belong.

Tonight, he saunters beside me into the crowded venue, dense with stylish people of (obvious) color. Beautiful Cherie waits. She's a good friend of mine from high school. Her skin is shaded sepia and I adore her. Noah used to flirt with her also. She used to tell me that if I were a boy, I'd be the perfect boyfriend. There is heat between us when Cherie and I embrace. She offers a mischievous feline grin and peels away from me, gesturing toward a Black man with high-cheek bones and a flat, expansive forehead. "My impromptu male escort," she tosses. I shake his hand and forget his name even after he repeats it. He seems eager to please her, somewhat nerdish. I take note that he's smaller in stature than she, knowing this makes him, ultimately, expendable because Cherie cares about these things, about looks. In her black cotton shirt, tall leather boots, and thigh-gripping indigo jeans, she matches many of the other women in the room. I wear an orange dress.

Cherie and her guy arrived early to secure coveted front row seats. Once our four bodies have settled into them, we let our smug chins wander, observing latecomers improvise comfort using dusty floors as props, carving elbowroom into brightly painted cement walls. The people who come here are cool people in cool clothes; they smoke long cigarettes, doodle in beat-up composition notebooks, cackle with their girlfriends, and tap shiny-shoed feet. The inhaling of gray fumes, the gray lead scratching marks, and the giddy giggling piled on top of the tapping create a sweet buzz that fills the air and replenishes me. A DJ spins and scratches furiously, sampling "One of these things does not belong." I glance at Noah. He smiles and mouths the lyrics. I cross my legs.

Six hours later, I step off a small stage with the open face of my poem journal clenched to my chest and a smile spread wide. Cherie and her date join the remaining ten café patrons—the regulars—in earnest, ego-boosting applause. Noah—now red-eyed and impressed—casually, confidently pecks my neck with his bright pink lips. "Would you like to sleep over?" he asks, impishly, preceding his "Good job." My softly spoken, "Yes," distracts him from my inching away; distracts me from the sight of my old high school girlfriend's heart pumping hard beneath her tight black shirt.

As we walk them to a towering hotel-turned-five-star-dormhouse, her nameless companion jerks Cherie's small waist towards his. She seems fluid but secure in his muscular arms and I must admit they look good together.

Cherie winks at Noah and squeezes my hand. "Get home safe," she sings. But I am not going home; not with a boy I love.

Time is a hyphen between Friday night and Saturday morning; we kill it beneath 42nd Street. The youthful living dead—spent from dance, spiraling out of ecstasy—make nightlife murmur around us. We notice then ignore each other; we wait for a slow, late train; we hum.

If someone hovers peripherally, it is an early dream; my drowsy delirium only. That the City harbors danger at this hour is laughable stereotype. Really, most people are harmless; really, most people could care less.

Our exhaustion renders Noah and I momentarily mute; this fatigue launches a casual lean into mutual trust. And here, I take him in: his shiny, curling black hair, cut yesterday, for me; his goatee kept because I asked him to; the shirt he wore three months ago when we—frustrated, feverish—fumbled; his missed fingers, long. My stare makes him fidget, but I dare not stop.

And if someone analyzes us—shifts laggardly beside us—it is, perhaps, deliberate, but not menacing, right? People are simply strange. Right?

The boy I do not love—but who excites me because he aspires to fuck me tonight—feigns a yawn that quivers wildly into laughter. "The first poet at the café?" he reminds, easing his way into seduction. I release my building tension with a giggle, nodding, remembering: her androgynous voice held us hostage as the trembling fingers of her pale right hand turned endless wrinkled white sheets on the music stand. Remembering, too: Her silly words! How they slipped out of her soft, stoned face as her white spit landed on the spongy part of the black, black microphone.

"Life is like an infectious blow job," she had said—Noah says now, grinning jesterly—"I don't spit, I swallow."

I cackle loud at our new shared memory and steal a glimpse of the dark, ghostly figure that has circled us three times now. I note that Noah hasn't yet noticed the cashew-hued Black man in the tattered navy-blue down jacket. His brows are thick with anger, I think, but I dare not peek again. *Because whatever this is, it's not about me. People have bad days.*

A distant drone catalyses collective sighs of relief. It is 4 AM when we board this train, finally. I keep my head low but the Black man—haunter, hunter—sits across from me. I sit next to Noah, of course, but not too close.

Groups of friends and romantic couples trickle into our car with their own conversations about bad poets. The train doors stay open long after they've entered; the train does not budge.

I tap my foot, impatient, and, against my will, heed two feet in grimy white sneakers tapping across from me. I stupidly look up to meet the Black man's vicious eyes. I look away and inch away from Noah who—seeing now, finally understanding—inches away from me.

But it's too late.

All sounds fade as the Black man speaks, "You owe me an apology!" He addresses Noah who is stunned, who has stiffened in his seat, who can only say, "Uh…I don't know what you mean, man."

Louder, as if an open mic just propped itself under his bottom bluish lip: "You don't know me, man, so you better watch it! You owe me an apology and I'm waiting for it." The vein in Noah's neck pumps so fast I can hear it. "Look—I'm sorry—" he says, swallowing, "but I don't know what you're talking about."

I survey the car for super-heroic or civilian intervention, but the groups and couples ogle each other like statues. Another train gusts in on the other side of the tracks. People push each other out of this loaded, stagnant car. People avoid my eyes.

Noah asks, calmly, "Switch trains?"

"Yeah" I say, rising, and we rush across, leaving the Black man seated behind us. As we exit, we hear the word "Faggot," above all hums. I tug on his sleeve and Noah does not take the bait.

We stand on the new train now, inhaling to exhale reassured breaths. But before the automatic doors slide shut, the Black man seeps through a slit and blows hot, heavy air into Noah's face.

"Yeah, that's right—what now? WHAT?" he screams. He's thin, but bulky, with amateur power. His hands are suggestively pocketed. His raised shoulders pitch forward—an onslaught, a shrug—to thump on the white boy's chest. Caught off-guard, Noah caves in, backs away.

The train starts to move, racing mercilessly down the tracks. Noah and I catch our balance on a silver pole gone dull, scratched-up and gray with too much touch. The Black man's lips curl into a sneer. We are trapped.

I watch the three Brothas seated to the right of me assess and dismiss me as adulterous. Two of them poke each other's ribs and stifle nervous laughter. The other one nods to the music knocking against his headphones. He raises the volume and closes his eyes.

No one else is in this car, save two crackheads at the opposite end. Fresh from a high, they bob; worn from guilt, I stare.

"Look—whatever it is I may have done to you—" Noah stammers and I wish he'd just shut up. Full of bass and boom, the Black man's voice interrupts, making it up as he goes along, "I don't even wanna hear it, man. You got five seconds to decide. One or two, fool. But either way, you gonna apologize."

He gently shifts a bulge in the front of his pants, but stuffs his hand back into his pocket before I can locate a ring. I look down at my shaky fingers: *Do I belong to him?*

Metal screams against metal as the unseen conductor forces this ride to express. Pulled by the momentum of the speeding train, the unconscious crackheads lean forward. The three Brothas are at the edge of their bright plastic seats also; glowing and delighted to witness a cathartic showdown between Noah and this angry Black man.

It embarrasses me to realize I do not know this stranger's name. It embarrasses me to realize I'm not sure who I would root for. I let my pelvis rise to meet the overused silver pole.

And here
there is death and poetry, poetry
about death. And there, so as not to laugh, I
concentrated
on that cheesy poet's thinning, graying
hair—how it slow-danced
with a warm breeze struggling
through a café vent.
And here now, if not a gold band or a diamond
what's the weapon in his pocket?
And shit, Cherie—without the heat between us—
or, better yet, her nameless escort
would be perfect for me right now.
And there, the DJ spun
so fiercely
but never—not once—played jazz.
For six whole hours, not even Coltrane.
No Holiday, Simone, or James.

No Miles, no Monk,
no nothing.
And here . . .

I am only actually staring at the Black man, but inside, I scat a requiem. And with this strong song-stare—my silent, screeching scat—I aim to poke his crusty eye out; I aim to scratch the stranger-familiar skin of his insolent, acne-worn cheek; I aim to be free of his random possessiveness with a solid kick to his groin. I aim to know him, also; to put my arm around him; to rock him with the violent love I feel sneaking up on me the way he crept up on us; I aim to be free of our shame. I cannot stop staring—won't stop staring—at the Black man who is teaching me that love, sometimes, is gibberish.

"Bring it on! I wish you would," the Black man rails, but with less steam. He looks and speaks to Noah, but jerks his hard head towards my lips. "I'd break your legs, you hear me?" he says, but he is backing away. "I wish I could break your legs," and for the first time, I notice his limp.

The train abandons its speed for a gentler, more settled rhythm. The Black man says it, deflating, "You're beautiful to me, Sista."

Noah swallows then whispers, "Let's go." I shake off my hesitation and follow him to the other end of the car. As we head toward the swaying crackheads, the Black man pulls his bare hand out of his pockets and takes steady aim at me. "Keep your white man, Sista. Keep him and protect him. Cuz he ain't protecting you. He can't! He can't." It is a sound like moaning. The three Brothas nod like apostles. "That's right," they repeat. "That's right."

Noah huffs and—suddenly eager to prove that he, too, wears pants—yanks my elbow like stern fatherhood. He leads me through sliding doors into the next car then through that car, past those doors, into the next.

The train stops soon at 96th Street. It is more crowded here, safer.

We see the Black man step off two cars away and walk quickly to increase the gap between us. The next time I look back, the Brotha has disappeared.

I meet eyes with every Black man we pass until Noah and I spill out of the subway. We walk where Broadway meets 116th, near his Ivy League campus. Noah self-consciously, but tenaciously puts a hand on my rigid back. Feeling his fingers makes me flinch, but trauma keeps me close.

After the silent ride in the elevator up to his small room on the very top floor—after the layers are peeled and we are ready to share his bed—Noah embraces me—shivering—whispers, "All that matters is I love you." Wordless, I peel away and press my thick lips to thin.

I will leave tomorrow, mourning.

THE BLIND TIGER OF LOVE

Thomas Hopkins

Years before tonight, back in college, Jane's boyfriend out of town, in the blind tiger of her bedroom, that same night they only made it through the first two acts of *Bringing Up Baby* on public television, a tired David untying a spent Jane from her bedposts, her fire burnt low for now, she asked him this: Remember when you shyly confided in me that you needed to listen to the *Kiss Me, Kate* soundtrack to fall asleep, and I said I could come over at night and sing you lullabies instead? Yes, David replied. Jane continued: Then you said, but then I'd want to wake up to the sound of your singing as well. And that was when I first realized that I wanted you next to me in the morning too. And then I was terrified, she said, that you were yanking my chain. David said nothing, just nestled into her fur, sank into her hide.

Tonight, at Jane's college roommate's wedding, Jane's and David's coats both wear a little shabbier for the years. Both have put more than enough champagne in their tanks, and it charges through their veins, knocking them off-kilter, nostalgic, and grinning, attempting a careful imitation of sobriety. David's wife is around the corner, seeking shrimp cocktail, and in a flash Jane covertly entraps his manhood, leans in close enough for necking, and whispers in his ear: I should have sunk my claws into you when I had the chance. You already did, thinks David, stiffening, blushing. Years ago you did, he thinks, and part of me's been trapped inside your cage ever since. Ah, no regrets, he says, winking. His wife returns with her plate. Got the last one, she says. Jane smiles, but only with her teeth.

HOMEWRECKERS

Kevin Sampsell

One of the girls next door was getting ready to move out. My wife and I thought they were lesbians but we weren't sure. Sometimes we heard moaning and what sounded like a bed frame quivering and knocking against the wall. They were big girls. Big knocking sounds.

Once I went over to ask them about an ant problem. An invasion. Neither girl was there, but their back door was open. I walked in to find another open door. A messy bedroom with sweat-stained bras slung over the brass doorknobs. Cups bigger than my fists. I listened to the silence whistle as I opened a dresser drawer. Stretched out panties and crisp condom wrappers. I heard a toilet flush.

My wife was doing sit-ups in the front room. She was naked. I entered with her morning coffee. "This is a nice view," I said.

"Thanks," she said.

"For the coffee?" I asked.

She took a sip and leaned her chest on her knees before resuming. "And everything else," she answered.

"Was that you last night? Out here? Making sounds?" I asked.

"No. Fell asleep on couch." Her sentences were short to accommodate her exercise. "Lesbians," she said between huffs.

"Those lesbians like their sounds," I said. I poured some M&Ms into a cup of yogurt and fingered my belly button. The fatter I got, the deeper my innie got.

"The ants are back," she said as she left the room.

"Here's how the ant kingdom works," said James, the maintenance guy. "The worker ants are sent out to find food for the queen. They find crumbs or whatever and take them back to where the queen is. The queen can be a big ol' bitch. Like, up to six inches long." He held out a measured distance between his huge fingers. There was a ring on one of the fingers that looked like it would cut the circulation off.

"You're not serious," I said.

"Oh yeah," he said, eyes getting wide like some UFO chaser. "Those queens can kill a snake or a squirrel."

"A squirrel?"

"Well, I saw one eat a hamster once." He pulled some small plastic circular things from his coat pocket. They looked like minia-ture models of the Superdome. "These traps have poison and the worker ants get contaminated and go back to the queen ant. The scent of the stuff in these things makes the queen want to breed, so she has sex with a few of her workers and eventually dies."

I couldn't help but imagine a weird ant porno—some tinny techno music playing over a poisonous insect gang bang.

Early morning. Too early to wake up. Maybe before six. A rhythmic thump came through the walls in our bedroom, jarring me from a dream. My wife had fallen asleep on the couch, but now she was up, ready to get in bed with me. Our TV set played a marathon of home improvement shows in the front room. I tuned my ears to the dull clunking, hoping I could hear voices or at least a sharp muf-fled scream or something. My sense of hearing was good in the dark. My penis was getting hard.

"What are you doing?" my wife asked from the doorway.

"Nothing," I said, eyes half-closed. I nodded at the wall. "Does that sound like lesbian love to you?"

"It's kind of a man's tempo, isn't it?"

The sounds stopped. There were no screams, groans, or exhales. My wife turned on the light. Blankets in a teepee-shape.

A couple weeks ago, James went home for lunch. He lived with his grandmother just a few blocks away from the apartment. She always cooked for him. Brown bag lunch. Most days, I'd see him eating lunch in his truck. But on this day, he ate enchiladas and watched a soap opera with his grandmother. He was supposed to be fixing the water heater in my quad but was behind as usual.

On his way back to work, he passed by a woman who flagged him down. He thought it was someone who needed help. He circled back around the block. On his return, he saw that she was an attractive woman, probably about thirty years old. He rolled the passenger side window down.

"Wanna have some fun?" she asked.

"Yeah. Um. What, uh, what are you doing?"

She fidgeted with the hem of her skirt and leaned over. She looked a little like an old girlfriend of his. "Can I get in? It's hot out here," she said.

James was nervous. He had never been with a prostitute before. He tried to remember what the laws were, the protocol. "Are you a cop?" he forced himself to ask.

"Let me in. I'll show you my pussy. That way you'll know I'm not a cop."

He unlocked the door for her. "I don't see too many girls like you out here," he said.

She got in the car and smiled at him. She lifted her blouse a little and pulled the waistband down on her skirt and panties. Her stomach was a little chubby. "See, I'll show you my pussy. See? I got a cute pussy."

James wanted to reach over and touch it but he just looked. He knew he still had to be careful. What would his grandmother say if this was one of those stings? If he went to jail? He thought if he didn't bring up money, he'd be safe. He hoped she was just a crazy person, a nymphomaniac. "Are you just like a, uh, exhibitionist or something?" When he talked to her it felt like swallowing. Half pride, half greasy air.

"Yeah, that's exactly it," she said. "So, what do you want to do? I could suck you off or we could fuck."

"What do you want to do?" James asked meekly.

"I want to fuck," she said. "I haven't been fucked today."

The neighbor girls sat outside, drinking and smoking as the sun went down. I could see boxes taped up and stacked in the front room. They had moved a few bigger things that day with a U-Haul.

It was hard to tell, really, if they were lovers or sisters or just friends. They looked a lot alike, but one of them had prettier hair. My wife and I never saw them touch. They talked mostly about their friends and said names we didn't know and used combinations of verbs that were unfamiliar to us. Our front door was open and some of their smoke had started drifting in. Suddenly, they were yelling at each other.

"You still don't know how to make eggs," shouted the one with nice hair.

"I had a shitty childhood," the other answered.

"You're not a kid anymore."

"Can't I just . . ."

And then their voices trailed off and hushed.

As they went back inside and closed the door, one of them said, "It's obvious that we all have our weaknesses."

A few hours later, sounds again through the wall. Were they singing to each other?

I even pressed a glass to the wall.

Then, with my free ear, I heard a siren. It got louder. It turned into my alarm clock.

My wife slept on the couch. Wine on her lips.

"I only do this once a week," Molly said to James. She had given him her name, right after she voiced her preference for fucking. "I'm a student," she said. "I just do this to help me pay for school. You have a condom, don't you?"

"No, sorry. Do you?" He wished he could just get to the sex. Just pull over somewhere and pound her in the backseat.

"This store," she pointed. "They sell singles."

He turned a tight corner, scraping and bumping a high curb. He parked in front of the mini-mart and rushed inside.

There were people standing in line. Someone buying a bunch of lottery tickets. A man on crutches with a case of beer. A woman behind him with a jar of salsa and a newspaper. James looked out the window and saw Molly waiting in his car, looking at something in her lap. He shifted his weight, feeling the swelling of his penis fade against his leg. Molly kept looking up, around. The cashier was slow, maybe actually retarded, mumbling something to the excited lottery ticket buyer. They both laughed. The man on crutches sighed and started to smell like urine and tobacco. James almost forgot what he was in line for. Self-consciously, he let the woman behind him go before him. Molly was smoking in his car. She took the air freshener off his rear view mirror and snuck it in her purse.

My wife was in the kitchen killing ants. Smashing them with a fingertip. I snuck up behind her and wrapped my arms around her, cupping her breasts. She ran warm water over her hands as I groped her. "What were you doing at the neighbors?" she asked me.

"When?" I said.

"Yesterday," she said, slipping away from me. "I saw you come out. What's that about?"

"They're lesbians," I said with a hiccup.

"How do you know that? Did you see them doing it?"

"No."

I didn't tell her about the one with pretty hair. I didn't tell her that I saw her crying. I didn't tell her that we talked. That we locked the door.

"What were you doing there?"

"Nothing. I looked around."

I didn't tell her that they were sisters. I didn't tell her about the hug. I didn't feel like telling her about how it felt. The soft body that let my fingers press in. Her name was Jodi. I let it stay in my mouth. We were quiet.

She dried her hands on a kitchen towel. "What would you be looking for?"

"Ants," I said. "I wondered if they had problems too."

James was breathing heavy, trying to explain to his grandmother. He was sitting on the couch. She was in her big rocking chair. "It was Dad's old girlfriend, Denise. She'd babysit me when I was eight or nine and tell me these stories about how she used to be a prostitute. The kind of things she'd have to do. It was weird. They were like adventure stories. I kind of liked them. Every time she'd talk about getting into someone's car, I'd imagine it like a kidnapping. Like she had to escape. Mostly it was about the escape, getting to the end of the adventure, walking away with the money. Dad didn't know she told me these stories. She also told me that was how she met Dad. When Dad was still with Mom."

The television was still on in front of them, the volume on zero. James sighed. He felt his words tainting the room, the photographs on his grandmother's mantel, the chairs, the brown carpet. He couldn't stand to look at his grandmother just then. His eyes went out of focus on the TV, blurry images that had no place in this private moment. His throat felt like it was closing, or flooding with sickness.

"She showed me things," he continued. "She showed me her female parts."

He heard his grandmother moaning softly. Tears came to him.

"Dad told me later that she was crazy. He said Denise didn't have any friends to talk to. But it was weird. Because I liked her more than most people. So I thought we were friends. She told me secrets and I saw something amazing in that. Dad never told me anything. There was nothing for us to share. When Denise left, I wanted to go find her, but I wasn't even old enough to drive yet. When I was old enough, I couldn't bring myself to drive to that part of town. I couldn't approach a woman like that. I always hoped that Denise or someone like her would find me, that they would pick me out."

He closed his eyes and felt his cheeks get wet. He covered his face and took a deep breath before he went on. "I'm just scared that I'll like it too much. Already, I feel like a different person."

From outside came the sound of his grandmother's cat fighting with a neighborhood cat. James got up to open the door. He called for the cat. He was glad for the distraction. He looked up and down the street, moving his stiff neck. He breathed in the outdoor air. The cat sprinted around a corner and ran into the house. It leaped into the rocking chair with James's grandmother. She woke from her sleep, startled.

The sounds were happening again. I had just fallen asleep and now I was wide awake again. I wanted to pound on the wall but held myself back. I tried to reason with myself. They were surely nice girls. They probably didn't know they were making so much noise. I looked over at my wife who was still sleeping with her mouth half-open and wet in the corners, eyelids twitching, one arm flopped over her head as if waiting for a teacher to call on her. I climbed out of bed and put some sweats on. As I was walking out the back door by the kitchen, I saw a swarm of ants on the counter hauling away big crumbs of cheese and Ritz crackers. I took some paper towels and wiped them into an open paper bag. I made sure to get them all, even as they tried climbing out of the bag. I could almost hear them calling out or screaming. From the bedroom, the knocking became louder and faster. I went outside with the bag. I cased the apartments, trying to see anything. Through one of their windows, I was able to see around the curtains and into the bedroom. The girl with pretty hair was lying there, reading a book. I couldn't see anyone else. It was quiet. Before I went back into my apartment, I put the bag of ants on the sidewalk and lit it on fire. After all the popping and hissing and smoke, I heard the banging again, coming from the bedroom.

The next morning, Jodi came over to ask if we could "possibly be quieter when it's late at night." I didn't know if she was joking or being angry. My wife laughed and told her that we were going to ask her to do the same. Jodi glared at me in disgust. My wife stopped laughing. We all stood there, thinking. I went to call James.

James arrived with a canister of ant poison and a tool belt heavy with blunt objects. "There's a way we can get in over here so that it doesn't actually damage your walls." He led Jodi, my wife, and myself to a place in the basement. "Sometimes we get varmits down here," he said.

I wasn't sure if he was totally serious about that. I thought "varmits" was a made-up word that country people used.

"Whatever it is might be more active at night because that's when it gets quiet. It might be sleeping right now," said James. "We've had raccoons before. It's possible that I may have to call someone else down here if that's what it is." He jostled open a small door that I guessed would place him somewhere under our bedroom. He turned on a large flashlight. "Stand back on that bench," he said, pointing behind us. We scuttled back and stood on the bench. The basement was full of other tenants' storage and some maintenance equipment like saws and pipes and paintbrushes. Someone had a warped pool table leaning against one wall, next to a taped-up poster of some teen girl singer I didn't recognize.

James stuck his head and shoulders into the square space. It looked like it was big enough for one person to crawl into if needed. I wondered if anyone ever stuck a dead body in there. James poked his head back out and coughed. He wiped at his eyes and spit on the ground. "Shit," he said, and stuck his head back in.

We all watched him and started to get a little concerned. "Is it safe to do that?" my wife called out. James stayed there, emerged a few seconds, then braced his foot on the wall and pushed himself up further. All we could see now was his left leg dangling out of the dark hole. A brief rustling sound was heard. After a minute, he lowered himself back out.

"It's right where you said it was," he said to all of us. He stood there like he was trying to think of something else to do. "Come look," he said, pointing just at me.

I walked over and scanned his eyes for clues as to what it might be. "It's okay," he said. "She's a sound sleeper."

I looked back to my wife and saw a look of jealousy, as if she wanted to be the one looking in this darkness between the walls. She turned to Jodi and said, "Men are so stupid." "Let the men get dirty," Jodi answered. "They all like to get dirty."

I stuck the flashlight in ahead of me. It didn't seem like dirt up there, really. More like a rough cement gutter, leading to tufts of sharp pink insulation. There was more room between the walls than I expected. After climbing a little further up I saw some movement. At first I thought it was a tail but quickly realized it was a trail of ants, an inch-thick army leading into a larger opening. I felt my feet searching for leverage and pushing against the wall under me. I tested a pipe for its temperature before grabbing it and pulling myself all the way up to see into the opening.

My eyes loomed wide and unblinking on the scene. There were dusty ant carcasses all over the place, males with wings torn half off and heads smashed gruesomely. In the middle of all this was the queen ant, the egg layer. She was about the size of my hand, sprawled—as much as you can imagine an ant being sprawled—on a mound of sandy-looking dirt. She didn't move or even flinch, even with a couple of males copulating with her huge thorax. One winged male fluttered softly around her head, also eager to mate.

I began to smell a brew of scents that arose from the busy colony. First lemons, then the musty smell of cheddar popcorn, then burned toast.

Some of the ants were fighting to get to the queen, crawling over others until they too could clutch her thorax for a few valuable seconds.

"Is everything okay?" I heard someone ask. Either Jodi or my wife.

The queen ant stirred a little then and began twitching. A number of eggs were expelling from her abdomen and oozing forth. Many of the males mated with her aggressively even as she did this. Here is where I noticed the knocking sound. It banged and echoed in the space where I was. I tried to cover my ears and noticed the queen leaning forward with her head pointed at me. I thought I could make out the eyes, golden green. It looked as if she were bracing herself or thinking. I stared back weakly, and for the first time, felt like an intruder.

SEX AND THE MARRIED DYKE

Lori Selke

Joan met Elizabeth at the company Christmas party.

Normally Joan was wary of office romances, but it was a big company. Liz worked in a different department with a different supervisor, practically in a different building. The company had to rent out an entire downtown hotel to accommodate all the party guests, most of whom Joan had never met before—including Elizabeth. This office romance was different.

Especially since it was Elizabeth who started it.

Joan had been contemplating having an affair for months. It wasn't that Joan didn't mean the vows she'd spoken on the back-yard deck, holding her partner Sarah's hand in front of their assembled guests. Five years ago Joan meant the words she said about commitment and engagement and dedication to making it work, and she still meant them now. Joan and Sarah as a couple were working, were soaring, it was giddy and delirious and wonderful in every way but one.

And it's hard to have an affair when you're a dyke.

You might think it would be easy, what with all the practice so many women had dancing in and out of closets at work and with their family—why not with their partners? But Joan's community was so small, so fueled by gossip.

Not that plenty of women didn't get away with behaving badly. The lone butch predator—every bar had one, and some had packs. These one-night stand specialists were notorious and known. But a one-night stand wasn't what Joan was looking for.

The lesbian one-night stand was a curious beast anyway. Lesbians didn't go in for nooners or booty calls or quickies in sleazy motels. Lesbians were oddly public about their sleeping around. If Joan started playing the wolf, word would get back to Sarah for sure.

Or maybe Joan was just an amateur and didn't know the truly secret spaces lesbians used for their illicit trysts. Maybe this explained the popularity of camping among her woman-loving friends. Maybe our national parks were full of cheating lesbian hearts.

Joan wore a tuxedo shirt and jacket to the Christmas party. Elizabeth was in a shimmery silver dress that clung to her pixieish figure. They met for the first time in front of the seafood buffet.

"Do you think I should try the oysters?" Liz said, gesturing at the huge shellfish display on ice. "On the one hand, they're free. On the other hand, do I trust this company's food safety?"

Joan smiled politely and shrugged, sipping at the flute of cheap champagne she held in her hand. "It's your stomach."

"I hear oysters are an aphrodisiac," Liz said, and suddenly it seemed that she was leering at Joan. She leaned in and whispered, "so's champagne."

"Are you coming on to me?" Joan said.

Liz giggled. "I might be. You look so handsome in that jacket, you know."

And that's when Joan guessed that Liz was straight.

What she didn't anticipate was that the flirting would continue all night, that Liz would follow her to the coat check, that she would swoop in for a kiss, that she would suggest taking a taxi back to her apartment.

For a while, Joan had contemplated placing a personal ad in the paper. But she never figured out what to say. Every lesbian personal ad she'd ever read was seeking exactly what Joan already had—comfort, romance, someone to settle down with. There were no raunchy dyke ads. Sometimes Joan perused the gay men's ads instead and imagined they were written by women, for her alone:

Need Older Horny Top

38, decent shape, horny, passionate, oral, bottom. Would like to hook up with a older horny top guy. Making out, cock sucking, and getting well fucked are some of my favorite things. Age, height, weight, race are unimportant. Cool attitude a must. I cannot host, but will travel.

Like To Make Out?

Me too! I'm into lots of kissing, body contact & oral action. Let's hook up at my place.

Wank Bud

Nothing complicated, just in and out hot wank bud wanted at your place. I need absolute discretion.

But if Joan perused the ads too long, she just got depressed. Friends with Benefits. Discreet Fuck Buddy Wanted. Hot Oral for Deprived Married Guys. It was all too much.

She would never have guessed that she would be seduced—and by a straight girl, no less. But dating a straight girl proved to be the perfect cover. Drinking and laughing at the bar? "Girls' night out." Dinner together? "Just good friends." Joan didn't exactly pass as a straight girl herself, but Liz was so disarming, that wherever they went, not even their co-workers suspected what was going on after hours.

And she was so beautiful, feminine in an unconscious way, not like the women Joan had dated before she met Sarah. Sarah was a granola dyke, with long hair and flowy dresses, and she never shaved her legs. Liz probably waxed hers. She definitely tweezed her eyebrows. But none of it seemed to bother her. She inhabited her personal style like a second skin, like the clingy dress Joan had first seen her in.

Joan had always heard horror stories about dating straight girls. How they never reciprocated sexually. How they would always break your heart. But Joan hadn't given Liz her heart, and Liz certainly had no qualms about touching her in bed.

"Are you sure you've never dated a woman before?" Joan asked, lying sweaty and panting on Joan's cotton flannel sheets one night when Sarah was out of town. "In college, maybe? Fooled around with your girlfriends in high school?"

"Nope, nope, nope," Liz laughed. "You've taught me everything I know."

In the spring, Liz cut her blonde hair short. Not too short. It wasn't like Joan's barbershop cut. It was still feminine, shaped around the ears, breezy. "Do you like it?" she asked.

"It makes you look like Peter Pan."

"Is that a bad thing?" But Liz didn't wait for an answer; she just laughed and twirled in place, running her fingers through her hair. "I like it. It makes me feel so much lighter and more free."

Ever since their first night together, Joan thought of Liz as essentially similar to a flute of champagne—helplessly bubbly, but with bite. But spring seemed to make her fizzier. And sweeter. Liz brought flowers to their next date— tulips, not roses. "I picked them up on the corner," she said when she saw Joan's expression. "I bought them for me as much as for you. I just thought they were pretty."

Liz began asking questions, too. Not about Sarah. Not relationship questions, exactly, either. "When did you come out?"

"In college." It was no dramatic story, but Joan told it anyway—how her friends had always been boys, how she tried dating one of them, how he suggests—gently—that maybe boys weren't her thing. He turned out to be gay, of course. They were still close; he'd been her best man. Joan didn't mention that last fact.

"Have you told your parents?"

"I invited them to the wedding."

Liz grinned. "Did they come?"

"My mother did. My parents are divorced. My father sent a card."

"So they were cool with everything?"

"I'd been dating Sarah for nearly ten years before we did it. I think they'd figured out she wasn't just my roommate. "

Liz dissolved into effervescent giggles.

It was only a few weeks later that Joan noticed a rainbow flag sticker on the back of Liz's car. She knew it was time to put a stop to things somehow.

Just as Joan hadn't been sure how to begin an affair, she wasn't sure how to break this one off. Would it be too cruel to just stop calling? What sort of explanation could she possibly offer? "I liked you as a straight girl, but not as a dyke." "You were safer when you liked men." "I thought I was special. I liked being unique."

She told herself it was just a casual thing, that Liz wouldn't mind. That Liz would come out, head to the bars, and every butch wolf would flock to her. Joan couldn't compete. Better to bow out of the picture now, like a gentleman. Let Liz sow her wild lesbian oats.

So she didn't call, and she tried not to think of Liz's face, laughing at the bar, crumpling into hurt. She could only imagine the latter; she had never seen it up close. There had been so little drama in their relationship. Surely this just underlined its no-strings nature.

She scratched Liz's name out of her address book with a ballpoint pen, almost tearing through the flimsy paper. She resisted the temptation to rip out the page entirely. Joan placed the address book on the nightstand next to the bed, and crawled under the sheets. Sarah was already in bed, snoring sweetly, her hair spread out against the pillow. Joan wanted to run her hands down the nape of her neck, along the collarbone, and into the hollow between her breasts. She wanted to reacquaint herself with Sarah's body, now more like a long-lost friend you see in the subway, whose eye you try to catch before they disappear again, maybe forever. But Sarah coveted her sleep, and Joan loved her enough to respect the long hours she worked, the early hour she had to rise. So she settled for a light peck on the forehead, a nuzzle behind the ear. There would be time for more some other night, Joan hoped. She wasn't going anywhere.

BREAK-UP SEX

Eli Brown

without a condom
on the stubborn edge of the bathtub
because she was bleeding

sweaty and grunting like the time
we moved all of our things
into one home

the red was everywhere
when we finally separated
we both gasped

it looked like
without either of us knowing
I had killed her

> *ok yes I fucked him*
> *is that what you want to hear*
> *everything I've said is a lie*

maybe if we do it this way
this skin in open skin
there will be a burst

like the golden bubble of caviar
breaking in the mouth
and we will be sharing the same blood

a new creature with eight limbs
scrambling on the grisly porcelain
pressing its smitten halves desperately together

THE OTHER MAN
Stephen Elliott

Before the home to wreck and the decision that leaves me naked and alone at the foot of my bed, there's Wilhelmina. The first time I meet Wilhelmina it's at the back of the giant singles bar known as the Internet.

The first time I see her face to face, she asks, "Do I look okay?" She wears white slacks and a white jacket over a tan shirt. Her face is long and unhappy. I think she is beautiful and I say so. "Do you have a problem with black women?" she asks. I say, "I don't think so." We talk for just a couple of minutes before she leaves for work. I have taken the train to meet her. I am an hour away from home.

The first time we break up she hits me with a whip and my back bleeds and there will later be a small scar. "Do you know why I'm angry at you? Because you don't make time for me."

She draws all over me in non-toxic permanent marker, Whore, Slut, Pig. I am going to a reading and she is going on a date.

"Don't go," I say.

"You said you had a reading to go to."

"Don't."

She lets out a long sigh and says she will be back later. And that's when I use my safe word, which I've used only once before, when I thought she was going to tear my rotator cuff.

"Are you safe wording the scene or the relationship?" she asks. If I had a rewind button, I would go back and tell her I was safe wording the scene. That I wasn't comfortable going out in public with all of the things she'd written beneath my clothes. That I keep my life carefully compartmentalized and if things started to blend together I would fall apart. That she could do whatever she wanted to me as long as she was there. But I don't say any of that.

"You broke my heart," she says when we get back together in a bar below San Francisco near the airport. "And it can never be fixed."

I put my face against her shoulder and apologize. She runs her finger inside my collar and assures me it's too late. But she doesn't tell me about the other guy.

She tells me about "other guys." There is a semi-professional ice skater, a computer consultant who wants to be a painter. She tells me each one's worst trait and I make fun of them and she likes that. But I am starting to get jealous. I am on the road a lot, writing about an election, and when she reads an article of mine where I joke about flirting with someone on the campaign trail, she freaks out.

"If I ever catch you with someone else, I will destroy her face. I'll kill her. Do you hear me?"

"I'm having a really bad week," I say, trying to deflect her anger.

"This isn't about you," she says. "Think about me."

She's right. I put myself first too often. "Alright. I will. I'll try to make your life easier, not harder."

"You hurt my feelings," she says.

"I love you," I tell her.

"I love you too, asshole."

I think she is making me a better person. It's deep in winter and I'm in New Hampshire. John Kerry speaks on a three-foot platform but I can't understand anything he says. Outside is a bridge and then the twisted alleyways and industrial buildings of Manchester. The presidential candidates are running their campaigns from makeshift lofts in the factory district. The lake is frozen.

These are my memories of Wilhelmina:

- She comes to the city for the first time and we have dinner. In a cab back to the train station she says something mean and I'm embarrassed because I'm not used to being in public with a dominant woman. It's our first real date and I don't think it went well. Before boarding the train, she grips my vest and kisses me on the mouth.
- I'm tied beneath my clothes and the rope is limiting my movement. We're in a restaurant near her house and I ask the waiter if I can have another beer. "Ask permission first," she tells

me. From that point forward, I don't look at menus and she orders all of my food for me when we go out.

• It's wet and cold in San Francisco. She's been hitting me and I don't care. I'm tired of it. She's always angry with me. It's gotten predictable. She's pinning my arms with her knees. My face is burning and red. She's wearing blue jeans. "I'm not your father," she says angrily. "I'm not your mother reincarnate." I can't stop crying. I cry for hours.

• Wilhelmina asks if I would love her if she were fat and ugly. I tell her I don't know. "I'd love you," she says. But we're not really talking about fat and ugly, we're talking about old and sick.

• I complain that I'm lonely on the busses. The other journalists won't talk to me. I miss her so much it hurts. In response she emails a picture of herself in bright red lipstick wearing a latex bikini and latex gloves covered in a body fishnet. "Just remember," she writes, "if the urge to show this to anyone ever strikes, I have pictures of you, too." Behind her, a man is fiddling with the jukebox. He's wearing leather chaps and his ass is naked.

• I'm in wrist cuffs and a collar. Early in the morning a triangular shaft of light spikes through the curtains. I'm awake and staring into her hair, thinking of my list of tasks for the day. She rolls over and clips my wrists to my neck. Then she goes back to sleep.

• Her smell is like flowers. It's the most wonderful smell I've ever encountered, and every time I see her, I can smell her for days after.

"You have to leave," Wilhelmina says.

"Why?" I ask. I have given up my apartment and not yet moved into my room in the Mission. I travel on campaign busses and live in hotel rooms. My head is swirling with promises made by politicians who have no intention of keeping them. Wilhelmina's apartment is always clean and she has a king-sized bed. We've been together in our strange way for nine months and I've decided I want to spend the rest of my life with her.

"Someone might come over."

It's midnight and I weigh what she is saying. There are several possibilities. One is that she has been on a date with someone who has turned out to be dangerous and he is stalking her. But she won't tell me. She's tight with information when she wants to be.

"I'm not afraid of him," I say.

"You should be. He's bigger than you."

"No," I say. But she's already out of bed.

"C'mon. I'll give you a ride."

"I don't want to go," I tell her, putting on my clothes in her foyer where they have been folded into a pile on top of my backpack. She sits in her chair near the window, looking nervously outside. If something's worth having, it's worth fighting for.

"You said you wanted to make my life less difficult," she says, rubbing her eyes.

Walking down the street, looking for a bar and a drink, I remember my ex-fiancé, and how after we'd broken up she started dating a good friend of mine. And how I walked away not just from her, but also from every friend I had made in college. Then I think of my best friend growing up and how her desires were similar to mine and she finally found someone to beat her and protect her, but her boyfriend won't allow her to see me, and I haven't seen her in years. I give up on things too easily.

At 19th and Valencia a young woman in a Honda swerves to the right then cuts back across the median and collides with a yellow cab. The two drivers get out. "You hit me from behind," she tells the cabdriver, an Arab in his late forties who is working the graveyard shift, squinting at his front grill. "It was your fault." I wait outside the convenience store for the police to arrive then I tell them everything I know.

Wilhelmina is in a serious relationship with someone else. But I'm not ready to let go. I see her later that week and we don't talk about it. But then I have to leave. Howard Dean is staking his entire campaign on Wisconsin. I have a contract. I fly into Milwaukee for the last stand alone primary of the season and stay in the Milwaukee Hilton, an enormous red building with a wire sign on the roof. From the highway, the hotel looks like a gargoyle with its wings folded into its brick chest.

Two months later, Wilhelmina breaks up with me. She says she needs to give her other relationship a chance. We exchange accusatory emails. She blames me for breaking up with her the first time and for always being away. She says I am inconsistent. I tell her I don't buy it, because she has always seen other people. I don't see what makes this special. A month later we are back together.

"You can't come to my apartment anymore," she tells me. "He has the keys and he's moving in."

I know who he is; I saw a letter addressed to him on Wilhelmina's coffee table.

Our final week together is climactic and ends with a whimper. She picks me up at the racetrack, crying. She feels forced to make a decision she doesn't want to make. I know we are unsustainable and her other "vanilla" relationship has to be better for her. But I can't let go. I keep telling myself, I was there first and this other person has no right to come between us. I don't want to be a coward anymore. I don't want to lose something important again. I am old enough to know you can't always get things back once they are gone. Second chances are a myth perpetuated by optimists and con men and I don't want to be the fool.

She sits in the passenger seat and doesn't stop me when I reach over and pull her dress up over her knees. As we drive past the South San Francisco hills, we talk about seeing a movie but end up spending the entire day in bed.

"I'll live with him but I'll marry you," she tells me on our last night together. "You need to be ready for me to show up and move in." I'm drinking and I say I don't want her to live with him. I want to go back to her place with her down comforter and her giant bed.

"You need to decide if you're in this for the long haul," she tells me. "I don't want to waste my time." It's a dark bar and I focus on the beer sign in front of me, its smooth green light imitating a river.

"Can I answer you tomorrow? I don't want to say the wrong thing." We've been together two weeks short of a year and I know her temper. It's like my father's temper, explosive and all consuming. And, like my father, she will go until you break and then shower you with love until you feel better.

It's just a matter of time. I can win. She doesn't love him. He found her handcuffs and thought it was a phase she went through. I know about him but he doesn't know about me. At some point, he will find out about us and that will finish them. All the signs point in my favor. She told me she was tired of being alone.

The end is simple. She is opening my bags, going through my papers. It hadn't occurred to me that I would be caught first. "You shouldn't do that," I say when I realize I don't know what is in my own bags.

"Why?" she replies. "Are you hiding something from me?"

I don't answer. I have always hidden things from her. The marks on my side spelling her name are already hardening into long, thin scabs.

I sit in front of her with my head in her lap as she reads through my book sales, my notes from the campaign trail, and then a detailed multi-page exposition of our date at the track just days earlier.

"What the fuck is this?" she asks. I look up at her hand holding the pages. Her long fingers, her chin.

"It's just notes," I say. "It doesn't mean anything."

"Why does it say chapter six on the top, then?"

It sounds funny but it isn't. It's the end: a breach of trust so staggering, so complete, as to be insurmountable. "You make this so easy," she says. Later that night, I get a note from her: Don't email me. Don't call me. Don't write about me again.

But I'm not capable of not writing about her for the simple reason that I loved her. I can't keep that to myself. It's selfish, but I never made claims to nobility.

You could ask, in this case, who the homewrecker is. The answer might be that Wilhelmina and I never had a home to wreck. Yet, somehow, I know that the real answer is that I tried to wreck someone else's home and failed. The pieces fall together and form a picture as clear and obvious as the contours of mountains. There wasn't anybody between Wilhelmina and I. I was always the other man, lying in wait to destroy something I couldn't have.

PROTECTION

S. Bear Bergmann

In a whore's bedroom I inspect
the talismans. Every time.
Tiny boxes wrapped thought-tight
with hair, or else containing
the desiccated remains of
I-don't-want-to-know-what. Statues
of the Virgin, mostly glam Latin versions
with Dia de los Muertos dolls
guest-starring in the creches. Collages
that flow over their frames, seeking light.
Broken jewelry. Almost always
some glitter, almost always
some blood. One day I asked
Anna-Louise what they were for?
She wouldn't tell me.
I started asking; Tasha says hers keep safe
the secret of her true name,
Katie says hers avert violence.
But Josephine says these too are lies,
that every whore's chamber is guarded
against the wrath of The Wife. They curse
these girls I love for an hour at a time,
that scorn of a self-righteous woman keen
as a cold wind, and just as unwelcome
at the door. I tell her I'm single; I carry
no harm across her threshold. Her glance flickers,
she says softly:

"Not yet."

Then she starts unbuttoning,
but she's naked already.

STALKING GOD

Gina Frangello

Suddenly, Jayne is afflicted with acne. It makes no sense; she is thirty-three. The same age as Jesus Christ, as Blaine keeps reminding her. In high school, her face was clear, if a bit ruddy, like her mother's. Mom gave Jayne big bones and red cheeks and a Polish nose that looks innocuous at a glance but on closer scrutiny resembles a lump of Play-Doh. Jayne would like to blame Blaine's waning interest on the inexplicable hormonal disaster playing itself out on her skin. But let's face it, before Blaine, she had not had a relationship, gotten laid, or gone on a date—even a bad one—in five years. Plus, lots of ugly people are married and most married people are ugly. So she has no choice but to blame her personality.

Mom, meanwhile, is swinging from the proverbial coital rafters with some married hypocrite who works for the Archdiocese of Chicago and is never going to leave his wife. Which is only fair, since Mom herself works for the Archdiocese and is married to Marty, Jayne's Jewish stepfather, who she does not intend to leave because it would be "too expensive." Jayne cannot recall what horrible utterance on her part prompted her mother to reveal this torrid affair—over the phone no less—but since, Mom's confession has resulted in her calling Jayne daily like a best friend from junior high. Mom calls with some veneer of advice about how to stain Jayne's dining room chairs or a new use for fat-free Kool Whip, and ends up offering cringe-worthy details from her love life. It is, truly, too much.

Blaine says that Jayne likes to cast herself as the tragic heroine of her own life. But what sane person would not be upset that her fifty-something mother surpasses her in feminine wiles, and is bonking some fellow Catholic and just begging God to strike them dead? As if marrying a Jew was not rebellion enough. Her mother is the black widow. Her mother has black lingerie. Jayne has zits and increasingly feels like live veal in the cramped, dark box of her apartment, waiting for her phone to ring. She has no tangible reason other than pride not to wear briefs with holes around the elastic waistband.

So come on.

The phone rings at work. Jayne cradles the receiver in the wool of her sweatered shoulder, chirps like a Stepford Wife, "St. Xavier's Day School, how can I help you?"

"Honey," Mom says. "You sound thin. Let me take you to lunch."

"I . . . sound . . . thin?"

"Wan," Mom clarifies. "Insubstantial. Peaked." If she'd had the money to attend, her mother would never have dropped out of college.

"What do you say? I'll pick you up so I can say hello to everyone."

"Whatever. I can't be late back to work like last time—the fundraising auction's on Friday night, I'm swamped."

"See you soon then!" Mom sounds breathless, like a porn star. "I can't wait."

"The stigma against infidelity is more about honesty than about sex," Blaine said the first time he told her he was not "into" monogamy. "It's an issue of one illegal fuck making future acts of deception easier—you get acclimated to lying, so pretty soon you don't just lie about big stuff like where your dick was last night, but anything, like where you work, how much you drink, what you ate for dinner. It's like you have to stay in practice. Deceit's rough. That's why I'm up front—I cut all that shit off at the pass."

It was typical of Blaine to twist everything so that the partner being cheated on (a la Jayne; a la Marty) became an irrelevant sidebar to some broader, esoteric moral question—one that somehow spit him out smelling like a rose atop a pile of misguided bourgeois turds. Now, watching Mom waltz into the Day School on the arm of a stiff-backed, salt-and-pepper-haired facsimile of J. Peterman from Seinfeld, Jayne's nostalgia for deception and repression is as sharp as cardiac arrest—has Blaine gotten to Mom too?

"Sophie," booms Mom. "This is Lawrence. Larry, this is my Sophie Jayne."

Jayne mouths, "Uh."

Beaming with the authority of a woman with her husband's checkbook in her handbag and her lover's semen warm and glowing inside her, Mom says, "I've so wanted you two to meet. Let's splurge and go to Season's. Sophie, they have lots of healthy, low-cal options."

Lawrence holds the door open for them, also grinning—he is an argyle-and-toothy breed: executive jocular. He doesn't look religious. He doesn't have the same weird, rapturous vacancy in his eyes her mother often wears, or that breathy voice so common in holy women, the Carl Rodgers counselor-speak so common in the men. He looks like an extraordinarily subtle car salesman, or a politician's sharkish brother. He looks like the kind of man you can immediately imagine owning a penis, a phenomenon both disquieting and rare. Jayne takes the door from him, stands with its knob in her hand until he slinks forward to join with her mother. With the heavy-footed trudge of her adolescence, she trails them to what she is certain will be a shiny silver luxury car.

"Hurry up, Sophie. You're the one who doesn't want to be late!" Mom reaches, without thought—always without thought—for Lawrence's hand; Jayne nearly covers her eyes. But no, it is over, they will not start making out right here on the street: Lawrence, out of some vestige of shame, perhaps from his pre-adulterous days, has oh-so-subtly pulled his hand away.

Snapshot Nine. Dad: suede, fringed "draft dodger" jacket, red bandanna barely visible below new, jauntily-angled cop's cap, mouth open from singing "Magic Carpet Ride" by Steppenwolf, unidentifiable bottle in wedding ring hand resting on Formica counter.

Subtext: Mom chose this as the photo to be displayed. Though Dad's relatives don't like it (Sophie has heard their whispers for three days straight), nobody said anything because Mom is the one who found Dad in the bedroom with half his head blown off, and they all agree this was "traumatic," though none of them can seem to bring themselves to get near her. They keep staring as though she pulled the trigger. At the luncheon afterwards at Red Apple, Sophie is invisible and bored. She sits under Dad's sisters' table, watching smoke from their Benson & Hedges drift across the room, pretending to inhale on her straw.

Script:

"He finally confessed to Ma that the bitch was screwing around—with his own partner can you even fucking believe!—she had the gall to ask him for a divorce just three days before he . . . I mean, he never even looked at anyone but her, not since he was fourteen. Jeez, plenty of my friends woulda killed to go out with him. That poor little girl, to have a mother like that, but I have to tell you, the kid looks so much like her, it's just . . . I know it's not right, but the sight of her makes me sick."

Jayne has not been home long enough to remove her shoes, has only just poured a Jameson's and downed one long sip, when the phone rings.

"Hey, baby." Glorious, half-drunk, New Orleans slurring. Blaine. "We still on for Friday?"

"Oh, um . . ." Has he forgotten that they have not seen each other in three weeks? Can casual heroin use cause amnesia? "I thought you work Friday nights."

"Oh, I get it, Diamond Girl," he says. "You have another date."

"No, I—" Stupid, stupid, should have said yes. "That's not what I mean."

"Did you have a bad day, baby? You sound stressed."

"A bad day? My mother and her lover came to take me to lunch."

"Oh. Cool. Is he hot?"

"Blaine, the woman has been married for nearly twenty years."

"So what you're saying is that she really deserves to finally have a little fun."

"So what you're saying is relationships aren't fun? That's why you're calling?"

"Girl, don't make me come over there and smack you around." He is smirking through the phone wires and right into her churning stomach. "I'm on till 2 AM tonight—do you have any idea what kind of whack jobs have need of a Kinkos past midnight? Don't give me a hard time."

The muscles of Jayne's face hurt with trying not to whoop for glee. "Six-thirty on Friday is fine," she manages. "I just thought you forgot."

The flowers she gave Blaine are still alive. She is momentarily stunned—nothing she has ever planted for herself lived out the week. He must be taking care of them like a mother bird, dropping food and water into their eager mouths buried under dirt. The soil is moist and cold—they will not last long; the weather is turning. All the petals are red, the color of love and drama and blood and passion and warmth: everything that matters. She knew he would appreciate that, but could not have guessed he was capable of such paternal ministering. The palpitations under her skin feel like disappointment, regret. Honestly, she had assumed that when she got here, they would already be dead. Though if that were true, why did she come?

It takes only seconds to yank them out by their roots: to turn this token of beauty into something ugly. She leaves the slack stems atop the raped dirt—looks fleetingly for some garbage in the yard of his apartment complex but finds it disturbingly clean. There, on the porch, is a weathered bag of salt—it must have been there since last winter; the bottom is corroded and leaking. She grabs a handful and smears it into the soil to kill all chances of renewal. Not only is it too late in the season to start fresh, but he'd have to go to some nursery and buy new soil, and let's face it, he would never, ever do that.

Snapshot Ten. Elizabeth: white off-the-shoulder blouse, newly-dyed red hair in Dorothy Hamill bob. Marty: Land's End button-down orange-and-white striped Oxford, Bermuda shorts, boat shoes, hair still clinging to top of head.

Subtext: Sophie Jane lurks behind the camera photographing Mom and Marty on their first date. Her grandmother on Dad's side, before she stopped speaking to Mom, always said that when Sophie got old enough to date, Mom should take a Polaroid of everyone so that if Sophie ever doesn't come home, the police will know what man to look for. Sophie wants to make sure Mom comes home, so she has become an avid photographer. Grandma did not visit but sent Sophie the camera for Christmas. Since, Sophie has photographed eleven men with Mom, each smiling, innocent. Mom has always come home, but none of the men ever show up again.

Script:

"So do you want to be a photographer when you grow up, young lady?"

Sophie doesn't answer. She stands with one leg on the sofa, the other on the coffee table, the camera in front of her face, bouncing up and down. In the viewfinder, Mom's head bobs like an apple.

"Sophie, Mr. Hirsch is speaking to you!"

Sophie stares, eyes dizzy. Mr. Hirsch repeats his question—then adds, "Or maybe an acrobat by the looks of it!" He chuckles at his own joke.

"I'm going to be a Satanist!" proclaims Sophie.

"Sophie!" Mom sounds terrified in a way Sophie did not think she had left in her. "Why would you say something like that to Mr. Hirsch—or to anyone for that matter?"

"Heaven's just a bunch of harps and junk. Nobody cool goes there. I'm going to be a Satanist so I can go to hell and see my dad."

Behind the camera's lens, she watches her mother's face grow larger in the frame, becoming only a nose. Mom's rings against Sophie's cheekbone make a muffled, crunchy sound. Mom has turned on her strappy sandals and raced up the stairs, already sobbing. Mr. Hirsch stands with Sophie, whose Polaroid has thudded to the shag carpet. She cannot hear Mom anymore, but knows she will be upstairs sprawled across her big bed, shoes dangling off the edge, door locked; Sophie will never get in tonight. Mr. Hirsch will have to go home; like the others, he will not be back.

"Sweetheart," Mr. Hirsch says, gathering Sophie to the couch, pressing a warm, dry hand against her pulsing cheek. "I'm sure you didn't mean to upset your mother. She loved your dad very much and she doesn't like to hear you talk like that about him, even as a joke. Do you understand?"

Sophie wants to lurch from his touch. On the table, two photos brighten in tandem, developing into something already out of reach. The camera needs to die now—she will smash it with a rock, throw it out a window, something. As soon as this man leaves.

"I'm sorry, Sophie." Mr. Hirsch does look sorry, and Sophie is surprised. "Sometimes it does help to laugh at our losses. I know you're doing your best to cope. You shouldn't have to deal with such difficult, adult things at your age."

"Suicide is a mortal sin if you're Catholic," she explains patiently, like her fourth grade teacher discussing fractions. "Mom cries about it all the time on the phone to Father Hardigan." Sophie leans over and hands him one of the photos. Maybe he would like a souvenir of Mom, since he will never want to come back again.

They swap: his American Spirit for her Dunhill Light. Light their cigarettes off the candle burning at her bedside. The black hair of Blaine's body stands out like ink on her cream sheets. Jayne leans back against the wall—there is no headboard and her head hits the bottom of a framed Matisse above the bed—and inhales, tries to look casual.

"Look at you, posing," says Blaine. "You can't wait to get dressed, can you?"

He does not permit her a moment's peace in her pretenses—she remembers that now, how uncomfortable it makes her. How it kills everything in the moment and only makes her love him more afterward. Jayne flings back the sheet and walks naked—what the hell do naked people do with their arms?—to the armoire and gets out the decanter of Jameson's.

"Do you care for a drink? We can take it on the balcony."

Half of Blaine's mouth turns up. "Like this?"

"Hell yeah."

"It's September."

"Oh, that's right Southern Boy. You're a weather pussy."

But in the midnight air, her pale skin glows conspicuously—he is at home in the darkness. She has never put any chairs out on her balcony; the cement is chilly on her ass. Soothing. No stars are visible—the lake is indistinguishable from black air. This is not even a balcony, really; there is no rail; it's just a slab of cement that you have to crawl out a window to access. The management planned to make sliding doors but then changed their minds—cheaper, no doubt, to go without. Jayne scoots closer to the edge, says, "Wanna give the neighbors a show?"

"What neighbors? I don't think anyone can see us here."

"Them." Jayne points a finger down.

He perks up: a little boy, curious, eager to think he can stir things up. "How?"

And then she is hanging, breasts flopping upward toward her chin, the edge of the cement pinching into her stomach. From above she hears Blaine's "Whoa, shit!"—she's swinging upside down, legs and hips still steady on the slab above, straining to reach the window beneath her own. The lights are on but she doesn't see anyone inside. Knuckles barely grazing the glass pane, she knocks.

"What the fuck are you doing?" Blaine is pulling at her legs. No—knocking her off her balance; the weight of her top half tipping her forward—she squeals, "Let go!" but he has yanked her back, cement scraping the tender skin of her abdomen. She lays naked beneath him like a fallen angel, twisted up to shield her wounds.

"Why did you pull me like that? You could have killed me!"

"Are you out of your mind? You could've killed yourself."

"I've done it before without anyone here. I love heights. I'm not afraid."

"Whatever, girl." He is bored with it already: nobody defying death, nobody to rescue. She is not appropriately grateful. She suddenly wishes for her clothes.

"Thanks for trying to help, though."

"Uh-huh." His ass cheeks parting as he climbs back through the window strike her as less vulnerable than sinister; animalistic. His nudity seems cloaked by hair, while she is truly naked. Even with all his lovers, he is insecure—confided once that he hoped to have electrolysis done on his back once his paintings started to sell and he had some cash. Though he's thirty-five and has only shown his work in a couple of amateurish neighborhood galleries where people came for free wine and didn't buy anything, Jayne trusts he'll be famous someday, if only because she won't be at his side to enjoy it.

By the time she joins him, he has pulled on his underwear and trousers. He is dressing jerkily, agitated—she has never seen him anything but languid before. Desperation rises . . .

"Blaaiine. Look, I'm sorry I scared you. But I mean, you of all people should understand. It's just a high, that's all. It's like drugs, only I like it more because I can control it."

"Sounds to me like you're trying to die but don't have the balls to kill yourself."

"Jesus, don't be melodramatic. I could say the same thing about you!"

"Yeah, you could've." Almost sadly. "I'm working on changing. That's why I haven't been coming round too much. Nothing personal, but I got my own demons, you know." He tugs his belt too hard: "Ain't you heard, baby—*thanatos* can kill you."

Snapshot Eleven. Sophie: Paper-thin, yellowish-white cotton blouse of uniform from St. Benedict's, Gloria Vanderbilt jeans, hair in Dorothy Hamill bob; Refrigerator: list of ingredients for Bouche de Noel, drawing of Santa Claus with fangs, carrying a machete.

Subtext: The drawing is hanging for everyone to see because Mom is afraid of "judging" Sophie, which their family therapist warned her not to do. Though not visible in the photo, the caption beneath the drawing reads: "The legand of Santa is wrong because it tells kids that Christmas is about greed and getting espensive stuff instead of about the birth of our Lord. Santa Claus is vialente against Jesus's message. Instead of a uzi or a very sharp knife, I would just like some Tropical Fruit Life Savers and Peace On Earth. Merry Christmas to all from Sophie Claus. Mom had thrust the picture at their therapist, exclaiming, "She thinks her last name is Claus now—she must think her father turned into Santa Claus after he died—I think she's in denial!" The therapist explained that Sophie was actually trying to take a positive step in improving Santa's integration into the Christmas Story by recasting him in her own image: a peace-loving girl with simple, nonmaterial desires. The therapist likes to make a lot out of things—imagine complicated meanings—otherwise she would go nuts talking to so many people about their boring problems. After Mom left, she asked Sophie to draw a picture of her father and write him a letter. Sophie's picture was of a horse grazing in some flowers.

Script:

"Do you see your father anywhere in that field?"

"Mom's boyfriend, Marty, took me for a riding lesson and I was drawing it for Dad," Sophie explained. "Dad used to draw horses when he was a kid. He should have gone to art school, Mom says, but he didn't have any money. He never rode a horse—he just knew what they were from TV. He'd be glad I could have riding lessons cause he must've always wanted them and parents like their kids to have the stuff they wanted. They're happy to sacrifice themselves for it, like Jesus sacrificed himself for our sins."

Jayne waits until Mom has finished one glass of sauvignon blanc before she quips, breezily, "So I have a boyfriend."

Mom's face brightens in that vacant way. "I thought you already had one, hon."

"No, I mean, well . . . yes, I was seeing someone, but now it's serious."

"Oh?" Same brightening—if Mom gets any brighter she will burn herself out. "Is it that starving artist? Bain Gun?"

"Blaine Cannon!" Giggles erupt; Jayne decides to believe Mom has made a joke. "He told me the other night, after the St. Xavier fundraiser, that he's trying to change—he's had kind of a wild life—and now he wants to settle down."

"That's wonderful!" Mom is leaning across the table of RL, flagging the waiter down and ordering another round of wine. "Though men never really change—you know that, don't you? It's cute when they offer to try, as long as the things they're referring to are only nuisances, not anything really bad, capital B."

Jayne is certain Mom would not categorize snorting H or practicing B&D—some of Blaine's favorite capital letter pastimes—as "nuisances." She smiles demurely.

"We should have gotten a bottle," Mom shrills, giddy. "After all, we're both in love . . . honey, didn't you think Larry just seemed like the warmest, kindest person? Doesn't he just radiate that?"

"Huh?" Jayne says. "Are you talking about that J. Peterman guy who says everything on cue, or about Marty?"

"Marty!" her mother scoffs. "Marty never says anything!"

"Maybe you're just not listening."

"Oh, Sophie Wee." Mom rests her hands on the tabletop, Christ-like. "Please. He really enjoyed you. He thought you were so bright . . . which, of course, you are." She studies the menu diligently, although she will have the soft-shell crab salad, obviously. Afterward she will drag Jayne next door to Ralph Lauren and offer to buy her an outfit, and Jayne will accept because she wants to blend in at work, and after that Jayne will feel as if Mom paid her off not to tell Marty, and feel guilty because the only reason she is holding her tongue is for fear that Marty will leave.

She stares around the dark wood room—it is meant to feel like a men's club in here, but all the patrons are women. In fact there are only . . . three men, she counts, in the entire place: all over sixty. Her mother likes this kind of vibe—likes to sit among ladies who lunch, although she herself works, works hard, harder than Marty wanted her to, harder than he works himself. But Mom knows—she was tricked once before: Never grow too dependent on a man. She will not give herself up this time. Maybe she does not know how to give up anything anymore. Maybe that is the problem.

"Don't live with him," Mom warns abruptly, tone dire. "That Blaine. Divorce rates are higher among couples who live together. I learned that while training to be a Pre-Cana counselor. Modern couples tend to assume it's just the opposite, isn't that funny?"

"I don't want to get married," Jayne says, expecting her mother to gasp, but Mom is scanning the room—reassuring herself that she belongs here?—and only nods, so Jayne is not sure her words even register. She sighs.

"Mmm," Mom murmurs finally, eyes still on some distant goal. "I understand completely."

The voice on the other end of the phone is young and female, both of which come, stupidly, as a shock. "Can I help you?" chimes the girl—the manager who has been fetched to field a customer complaint. Behind her, the hum of copiers, white noise.

"I'm calling about a, um, person who works in the evening—to, well, about a man who works nights—I think he may be a manager. His name is Bain, something like. . ."

"Blaine Cannon, you must mean!" Such cheer—one would think this girl had cracked a major case for the FBI, rescued countless children. "Our night manager."

"Yes, well. Yes. Well. Mr. Cannon is sexually harassing his customers."

"Oh . . . wow. I mean, what do you mean?"

"It's pretty obvious. A woman walks in, she doesn't even have to be good looking, and he tries to pick her up. He's done it to me, so I sent one of my co-workers, married and twice his age, and he did it to her too. He called her baby and said he lived around the corner and wanted to bring her home to see his paintings. Can you believe it? Does he really think that's going to work on anyone who isn't totally desperate?"

"Gross!" The girl—she must be an earnest women's studies major, working her way through school to become a humorless, bespectacled professor in expensive tweed—takes a moment to compose herself. "I . . . God, I had no idea. I'm so sorry. If you want to come in and get some courtesy Kinkos cards, I mean, please, feel free—"

"I won't be needing any courtesy cards." Stiff, with an air of skepticism. "I wouldn't want to run into him again. I'll be taking my business elsewhere."

She hangs up before she can hear this contrite little co-ed—Blaine's probably banged her too—cross her heart and hope to die that a future run-in with The Kinkos Predator is out of the question.

Snapshot Seventeen. Jayne: Puffy hair, Bear's sweatshirt in honor of Superbowl Sunday, flowered Forenza jeans she used a coat hanger to zip; Marty: white T-shirt with faded (and passé)

"Where's the Beef?" slogan, lightweight blue Lands End cardigan, khakis, index and middle fingers in "V for victory" sign.

Subtext: Jayne rests her head on Marty's shoulder. He is her savior. As of their conversation last night, her underwear drawer is three hundred dollars richer; the abortion is scheduled for Monday. Mom cannot know. Mom would make Jayne have the baby and then give it up for adoption, and she cannot go through with that, she just can't. If Mom knew Marty had given her the money, she would divorce him, even though divorce is a sin too. Not like abortion, the ultimate sin—unless you count suicide.

Script: Marty did not raise his voice when she told him. He sat muted against the beige sofa of the TV room with Dad's Irish Setter asleep on his knee: A portrait worthy of Mike Brady. He said, "Does the father know about this?" and Jayne yelped, "God no!" then chewed her lip. This perfect father she never had deserved better than a seventeen-year-old stepdaughter who got so drunk at parties she usually ended up sprawled on a guest room bed, underpants lost among a pile of coats, bra around her chin. Sometimes she didn't even remember the guy; she'd only find out at school when his girlfriend accidentally-on-purpose spilled coke all over her at lunch or wrote "whore" on her locker in lipstick. And so Jayne contemplated the right seed to have impregnated her: someone like Marty, a secret boyfriend she would martyr herself for by not revealing his name.

"I don't think it'd be a good idea to tell him," she stammered. "He doesn't want to be in a serious relationship with me because I'm not Jewish. We always use a condom, though—I don't know how this happened."

Marty nodded sagely. (Tonight, on a very special Brady Bunch, Jan gets knocked up by one of God's Chosen People . . .) "I've heard plenty of young men give that cop-out in my time. But telling him might make him think more seriously about his responsibilities. Sex is a big undertaking. There are risks. Not just pregnancy—"

"But we used a condom . . ."

"Emotional risks, Jaynie." Mom hated it when Marty used her new name. "Tell the truth. You love this boy, don't you? That's why you're trying to protect him?"

Jayne couldn't help it. Tears welled. This happened a lot—more and more—she believed herself.

"It won't get you anywhere, giving yourself to someone who doesn't want all of you. You're a wonderful girl. Don't hold yourself cheaply."

Jayne nodded. She had wrecked everything, every plan to redeem Dad. Instead she had abandoned him the moment she opened her legs; would seal his fate Monday. Her failure burned— she wondered if God felt sad too, or just wrathful. But Marty would give her the money. Marty would choose her over Mom. Even over God.

Through the keyhole, Blaine is wearing that same shirt he wore to the fundraiser. Instead of a jacket and tie, he has a vintage silk vest slung over it and has left it untucked over pants that, on anyone else, would look like basic cargo, but on Blaine manage to lend him the appearance of a gentleman guerrilla; Jayne half-expects to see a rifle casually slung over his shoulder. He smells like a jungle too—shuns deodorant as bourgeois. She loves his scent, wants to fling the door open and inhale his primitiveness. But with the way things have been going lately . . .

"What do you want?" she mutters through the door, half hoping he will not hear her and will slink away.

"Gutta show you something."

She inches the door open in slow motion; Blaine stands stock still, waiting until she's backed away to let him in. His good manners worry her. The way he is not checking out her cleavage worries her. His fingernails are stained with paint; he holds some crumpled paper in his hand.

"You probably already guessed as much." Voice low. "But I got a new old lady. I mean, not that you and I were ever . . . Yeah, so. Her daddy's a lawyer. She wants me to give you this."

Jayne moves forward to take his offering. Unfolds her fingers to find some kind of legal document, full of small print and blanks in which to fill in the names of parties. She sees her name typed in. Hands it back to Blaine. "What's this?" But she knows.

"So you'll stop the shit." His shuffling, guilty, shows he's been put up to this; instead of cheering Jayne, the knowledge that another woman wields such power over him when she held none is crushing. "I've known it was you all along, but I was letting it slide—I felt sorry for you, all that. I figured it'd be bad form not to accept a little rage. I guess I was flattered. But you pushed too far. I got fired."

Jayne's teeth clack together; her chest has gone so tremory her voice vibrates. "So you serve me a restraining order? For what? Suing me won't get your job back."

"It will if I can get phone records. It will if the day manager recognizes your voice. It will if you don't want to go to court and be forced to stay three hundred feet away from me like some psycho, so instead you come on in and tell my fascist boss that I didn't pinch some old woman's ass, I just dumped you cause you deserved it."

"I . . . what?"

"Come on, girl. Why're you trying to hold onto this game between us? I've been there, done that, you know? I need a little sweetness. Do you seriously prefer war to love?"

"Funny, I thought that was you." Tears roll—she wishes he would slap them away. Would he really sue her, humiliate her in public? A flash of memory: his hand, jerking her hair suddenly back to twist her face in his direction as she grunted on all fours. I'm the only person who knows what you look like right now. No matter what else we do together, I'll have seen your face at this moment, and that'll always be there. What would a man like that do with tenderness if he unearthed it? Yet on his face now, not a trace of enjoyment, no perverse pleasure in his victory; confusion fuzzes her brain like cotton. Wasn't it his goal all along to debase her? Isn't that what she wanted too?

"Ohh, I get it," she drawls. "You have some new, dew-faced young thing who doesn't like your not having a job, who figured out you're screwing around. So I get to be the scapegoat that brings you two together—you can burn me in the town square and she can sing "Stand By Your Man" while I fry—isn't that romantic? Well, I never did anything to you! I don't even know what you want me to admit to, but go ahead and hold your breath. See you in court."

He shakes his head, like she is a mirage he needs to clear from his vision. "I have your letters, Jayne. I've got, what, six of 'em, threatening me, berating me, telling me I'm going to hell—you're sick. Who else shoved a bunch of salt in my flower beds like my life is Sodom and Gomorrah? Who else calls ten times a day and hangs up—who wrote in lipstick all over my car about what a pig I am? The pitiful thing is, you really believe you're innocent, don't you? Do you even fucking see me, girl? Or am I some figment of your imagination?"

Nothing else to say. She slams the door and sinks to the floor, longing for a not-so-distant time when one Bette Davis door slam could spur a whole reinvention of events: that Blaine was stalking her like some Slacker of Darkness, that she needed Marty—always Marty—to come to her rescue. She imagines placing the call—Marty is Jewish; he knows lawyers too—weeping her version of the story, repeating threats that would soon sound so convincing she'd be able to envision Blaine's lips forming them. Marty would be at her apartment in a heartbeat; she could collapse into his arms; it would be so easy. With Marty she does not need to play saint, risk-taker, proper adult daughter in a serious relationship and a Lauren suit: basket case works better. If she's altered some details to protect him here and there, it's not really lying. Not like what Mom is doing.

It has always been only a matter of time before Mom grew tired of the way the line has been drawn in the sand of their triad. It has always been a matter of time before Mom would make sure—and what better way than to make Jayne complicit in the Lawrence affair?—that she loses Marty too.

Snapshot Twenty. One-bedroom studio: white walls, cracked ceiling paint, stained Berber carpet, decanter of Jameson's atop refrigerator, burgundy velvet bed covering, no chairs or couch.

Subtext: She has left her mother's home—although there are three empty bedrooms and no rent to pay—because it is the only way she can stop going to church. "As long as you live under my roof, you will come with me to Mass," Mom has said eight zillion times. Jayne feels giddy sitting with the giant *New York Times* at Café Voltaire on her first free Sunday, reading the stories from cover to cover and tinkering with the crosswords. She is a café-going chick who has known many dicks—big deal. She is a modern woman who once had an abortion—she has not committed any crime. She is no different from anyone else, not responsible for saving her father's soul through some misguided pitch at sainthood. She can drink in the afternoon. She can entertain any lover she wishes in her big, soft bed.

Only later that night does the bile begin to rise: the beginning of three weeks with her head in the toilet, unable to keep down food, unable to sleep without waking in sweat from dreams that Mom has died. Sometimes, instead of dying—victim of a bloody murder—Mom rejects her, turns her out into the street, mocking Jayne's threats of suicide, explaining, Don't you see? You're nobody to me—I don't mind if you die. At first, she attempts making it to class, to work. Although the bile pauses when she leaves the studio, her heart races and somersaults; her legs go numb. Behind her locked door, she curls on the bed the color of the inside of a heart and listens to the irate phone messages from her boss at Dominick's where she bags groceries, and to barbs from Mom who thinks Jayne is blowing her off. No one from UIC calls; it is a commuter school and Jayne has made few friends, none of whom would be surprised to find her cutting class.

She has lost thirteen pounds by the time Marty arrives at the door threatening to get the landlord if Jayne does not let him in. The sky outside is purple as a bruise. Marty gathers Jayne, who reeks—she can even smell herself—into his arms and rocks her while Jayne dry heaves onto his lap. With baby steps, he guides Jayne and her velvet comforter to his Volvo and helps her recline on the leather backseat. Mom greets them, wordless, at the door, her mouth a bitter, pinched imitation of itself. Alone, Marty heats Jayne's cocoa, makes up her bed.

In the mail, UIC grades arrive: all F's, even in the art classes. Nobody mentions her returning next semester. Instead, Mom gets Jayne a job at a Catholic preschool, whose headmistress is a friend of hers. St. Xavier's is full of everything that should make her feel better. At work, the staff commonly debates what to put in Christmas cards and newsletters, saying, "We don't want to come off as too religious." Most of the teachers are covertly pro-choice, pro-capital punishment; the Pope is akin to a charming but embarrassingly senile uncle only invited to dinner on major holidays. Yet the mediocre compromise of it all fits like a snug noose. So this is it then: one hypocritical foot in the faith that sears her, because she cannot stomach—literally—going cold turkey. Because neither has she any strength for sainthood; she prefers to drink herself numb, to smoke, and wear low-cut shirts. Religious guys leave her cold. Instead, assholes are what she's traded her father's soul for (they had all been "Blaines," right from the first.) She hates them: cheaters and users, seductive and cruel. They are the only ones able to move her.

Evenings, Mom asks about her colleagues and they gossip, eating cookies on the couch in newfound camaraderie. A feeling of fate washes over Jayne like a shallow river in which she is content to drown.

Script:

"I'm off to Mass."

"—"

"I'll pick up some lox and bagels for you and Marty on my way home."

Jayne glances up from the TV; Mom stands in the doorway framed by shimmery sun. Jayne wonders if she is sleeping around behind Marty's back. God will never forgive it, leaving the atonement of her dead father's sins in the hands of a woman like this. But Mom seems hardily prepared to shoulder the task, ignorant of her inadequacies and armed with the blithe righteousness Jayne associates with simplicity.

"Thanks, Mom. I'm starved."

Surprisingly, Mom answers the phone—she is hardly ever home lately, "working late." "Oh, sweetie," she chokes, voice dropping three decibels. "Larry says he needs time. He thinks what he's doing is wrong and can't live with the guilt, as though I'm not feeling guilty too. But don't I deserve to finally have love after all I've been through, Sophie? Your poor father and his depression, all those men who didn't want anything to do with a widow with three kids—anything but sex, that is—and Marty, well, Marty . . ."

"What's wrong with Marty?"

"Nothing, darling. He's wonderful. I knew he would be. Everything your father wasn't—I knew we were lucky to get him, that he'd be new hope for you."

"God, why do you always do that? Nothing's ever about me unless it lets you off the hook. Like you never loved Marty and only married him to be nice to me. Like that was ever even one of your concerns."

"Oh, Soph. You're a big girl now. Do things have to be so extreme?"

Jayne is quiet. It does not seem like the right moment—if ever there is one—to ask her mother whether she really slept with Dad's old partner, a rookie cop Jayne remembers having a wiry body and a pocket full of gum. Her father might have imagined it, as out of touch with reality as he was by the end. Jayne remembers the fights, the way her mother tried to hold his head when he said everyone was against him. Remembers even more clearly, only weeks before his death, the way Dad drove her to the police station when she'd been caught stealing taffy from the corner store: he made her sit in the back and turned his siren on, warned her about the rats in jail and how to make sure she kept the blanket over her head because they liked to nest in hair, until she . . . pathetic little Sophie . . . was crying so hard she hardly noticed Dad had turned the car around and was heading home without leaving her. So what if Mom succumbed to, even initiated, a fling with a cheerful, eager body? What was that compared to the fact that Dad never loved his own child—if he had, how could he have left her to strangers?

"Mom," Jayne says, because her mother, having said her part, is sure to hang up soon without asking Jayne anything about her life, sure there is nothing to tell. "Do you really believe that Dad is in hell? I mean, with what we know now about faulty brain chemistry and depression—clearly he should have been on medication, right? Do you really believe that his taking his life was a moral failure God could never forgive?"

There is silence. Perhaps some truths should never be uttered. Mom is breathing, making small noises that seem to be attempts at speech. Jayne bursts—she is crying again; she is so weak. "Well?"

"Sophie, honey, I don't know what to say. I can't remember ever having said anything like that. I don't know where you would have gotten that idea."

"But you said it all the time, to the priest, to your whole side of the family! How can you not remember? Besides, you're Catholic—isn't it implicit?"

"Darling," Mom says, and her voice is sad, but present, fully here. "I am a married woman having an affair with a married man behind my Jewish husband's back. What kind of Catholic do you think I am? I'm human, like everyone else. The year after your father died is like a fog to me—I was hardly more than twenty-five, with a child to support, and I'd never held a job. What can I say to you?" She sighs, the breath almost nostalgic. "It was another lifetime ago, Sophie. We were so, so young."

From outside, St. Benedict's church and school, near the house where Dad died, has changed. The school has been expanded and things look cleaner, newer; at the same time even the streets seem smaller to Jayne's adult frame. Inside, though, it is like walking back through time. She has heard the priest here is young now, hip. Jayne enters the dark foyer, averts her eyes from the holy water as she stands in the center aisle and takes a seat on the "Joseph" side. He is a father too—one who disappeared from the Bible, perhaps dead long before Jesus began his ministry. Did his son miss him? Earthly families were not supposed to be important compared with God, Jayne remembers. But God was not there to hold her head when she was sick; her body did not feel God's embrace. When Dad was writhing in his crazy misery, God did not magically change the workings of his mind to offer ease. God could not even cure Mom of her neediness for men—from her lust even now, in her fifties. Not "couldn't," Mom would say, "doesn't choose to." In any test of free will, Jayne's family has failed. If earthly detachment is a prerequisite to holiness, Jayne and Mom are fucked, both—they cannot stop thrashing, wanting, needing. It makes them hurt others without caution; they will do anything for a momentary salve.

She cannot call Marty and come clean, not about her long-ago pregnancy or Mom's affair. What father, what husband wants know? In lieu, she will call Kinkos and confess to being a woman scorned. She will quit St. Xavier's and look for a secular job where nobody knows her mother. Will ask Mom to stop buying her designer labels and pay for an art class instead. No—will get a night job to pay for her own class. She will do what her father never could: hold on to hope that things can change. That she can change too.

Or maybe none of these things will happen. Maybe her life is already too solidly defined, with all the endless monotony and disappointment of being an acne-prone, no-longer-young woman in a dead-end job with a botched education and a pox on her family's house: a life that does not always feel worth living. But if she is cursed, she will have to live with it because it is just too cruel, too unfair even for someone selfish and damaged, to cause her mother that much pain. And maybe this is the kernel of sanity and God that she retains, that Dad could not, and she will have to spend the rest of her life hugging it in her bed alone at night, nursing it like her one true light.

The incense here still lingers from Mass this afternoon. But Jayne prefers the nag champa she burns in her own apartment, the kind Blaine introduced her to—a smell so different from his smell, one that belongs to her even though he has gone away. She will not stay here long. But once, her father sat in this church, perhaps in this very pew with his teenage bride, both young and shiny and full of stupid, beautiful hope. She will remain just a little while, try to believe that she can feel him.

MAKING ADULTERY WORK

Merri Lisa Johnson

Sitting on the couch side by side, we face the bookshelf on the opposite wall of his office. Paul says something about our future, and I say something flippant and dismissive. He turns and asks earnestly, "So, you really think there's no way this can work?" I think about telling him the truth, the flat-out banal "of course not," and then decide against it. Instead I say, "Right now, sitting next to you, even though logically I am skeptical about our future, I feel that everything is possible and good." I feel warm inside this imagined space but also alone. I am lying and I know it. I know it will not turn out all right. I say it will anyway and blow hope into my hot tea.

I never told Paul this, but the truth is I picked him out as an adultery partner because I knew he was weak and troubled. I recognized that he was available the day he stood in my office doorway and announced that everyone liked his new hat except for his wife. We flirted over fundraising literature for juvenile diabetes. His son has it, and Paul has to check his blood sugar level ten times a day. The whole thing was textbook. Mostly, I just wanted to fuck. I fixated on him and played at having a crush, told my sister I missed him when I went away for a weekend. She said, "Be serious." "Why?" I wanted to know. "Feeling something pretend is more fun than feeling nothing at all." She didn't say anything else. I called Paul from my hotel room and announced that we should have an affair. He agreed.

I asked him about birth control. We hadn't even kissed yet. As I was leaving his office to go teach class, he stage whispered, "I love you." I stifled what I feared might be one of those off-key bird squawk laughs. My eyes got wide. "I love you too."

We spend long hours in bed with my windows open and coffee cooling on the sills. He tells me the smell of my breath changes at the moment of penetration, and the observation cracks me open. He touches my hip bones, calls them "iliac crests" and imagines sculpting me, pushes his thumbs into the hollows of my hips and asks me over and over, "Have you ever felt this way before?" I hesitate, remembering how hard I pined after previous boyfriends. I tell him he doesn't get to ask questions like that as long as he is going home to his wife every night. "Have you ever felt this way before," he intones. I reason inwardly that the question is vague enough that I can answer without exactly lying or putting him above the other men I loved more truly and deeply. "No. I haven't."

Paul buys tickets for a mandolin concert in Asheville and asks if I want to go. We sit and listen to Tim O'Brien. I put the ticket stub to the Orange Peel in a bone-encrusted box like a fetish or a piece of evidence. I was here. We swayed in sync.

I don't really like kids, but once you're in your thirties you have to be nice about people's offspring, so when Paul calls to invite me to watch him play Frisbee with his son, I drive to campus and smile on the early spring grass. The campus pastor walks by. A student with a crush on Paul comes and sits with us. She chats him up and I stare across the field. What am I doing here? I tell myself I don't know.

The best parts of the affair are when we are apart, and I am riding in my car with the Charlotte radio station on. I picture myself in pink spandex and sing along with Lil' Kim about givin' niggaz deep throat. I am elated and outlaw. The music is loud and I don't give a fuck about family values or protecting the nuclear family or being honest or finding my own man. I think of Paul coming over at 5 AM, picture him bragging he'll have me up early in the mornin' moanin', even though we are awkward, at best, in bed. I climb inside these rap songs and leave mild reality behind. I am pure joy and leisure and pleasure. Irreverent. When Paul leaves to take his son to school, I stay in bed and climax until my stomach muscles hurt. Then I head to the backyard, book in hand, where I work on my tan with bluegrass blaring out my kitchen window. Our relationship is never very good, but it flips a switch in me and I permit myself to be playful and erotic. I watch TV topless and keep my legs shaved. Gillian Welch wails that she's gonna do it anyway, even if it doesn't pay, and I shake my head mm-hmm.

I made an art out of making myself available at a moment's notice, trying to recreate the feelings I had in my passionate long-distance relationship years ago when I would fly to Seattle for a short weekend or drive to the airport in Ithaca through an ice storm just to prove how much it all mattered. In this case it only meant missing *Six Feet Under* and spending Sunday evening in a near-empty theater building with Paul while his wife thought he was grading papers.

One afternoon, we sit sparring over the question of what it means that he finally told his wife about us. I feel exposed, even though I had urged him to do it. I thought telling her would change everything, make him free, give me status. Official Girlfriendhood. But what it actually means is that she has more influence over when we see each other, and for how long. The phone rings. I hear him say to her, and indirectly to me, "I know you're going out tonight. We'll be home in a few minutes." Paul places the phone back on the hook, turns to me and asks if it's okay. I want to seem as sophisticated as I always meant to be, so I say, "Sure."

Ten minutes later, we are sitting at their dinner table while his wife gets ready to go out. I feel strange. I mean to be doing something fancy like "queering" marriage, but instead I am self-conscious and full of suspicion about why I am here. I would never have worn this purple flowered dress and blue sweater, or these black and pony-fur shoes, if I knew I was going to my lover's apartment tonight. I would have been chic in cotton cardigan and nondescript flats. Worst of all, I have forgotten to wear deodorant. As soon as she leaves, I ask to use their bathroom. Under the noise of running sink water, I open drawers and look frantically for some Secret. I push the off-brand stick underneath my tight empire waist seam and coat myself with the protective scent. When she comes home in two hours, she stands hip to hip with Paul, thanking me for coming, which is really a way of saying, "You can go now." I walk away, refrain from saying, "Who are you people fucking   kidding?"

For me, it was one orgasm in nine weeks. At least, only one while he was still there. I don't know how to explain this part, how I couldn't say, "Go down on me," and couldn't believe someone would wait seven weeks before doing it. He only did it once—right before his first marriage counseling session—and since I always have to fantasize to make it happen, this time it was like she was there, too: The image of her pushing the kitchen chairs under the table, wiping the crumbs from her son's toast into her palm and dumping them in the sink as she puts things in order and waits for Paul to pick her up to go save their marriage Go there with the smell of me on your face, I thought, and the picture broke open and ran down my legs. The theologian-slash-psychologist called me "this other gal" and convinced Paul he was playing out a childhood drama with me and his wife, and the slick gloss I left on his face evaporated like it was never there.

The last morning we saw each other, he was three hours late. I tried to stay under the covers like it was still dawn, but eventually I needed coffee and motion. He came into the kitchen and I glared with married eyes. I faced the counter and put sugar in my cup while he explained that he had spent the morning telling his wife the last of our intimate secrets—the 5 AM visits—and she kept him there while I cussed them both from across town. We couldn't quite force the intercourse once all the secrets were spilled, so I offered up a half-hearted hand job then stripped the sheets once he was gone.

Two years later and I'm still lying. Paul meant nothing to me. I never think about him anymore.

ANIMAL HUSBANDRY

Christine Hamm

The dog tells me that he's leaving me, that he no longer likes sticking his nose in my pussy. This last week he has been slipping his leash after I fall asleep and sucking cock in the back room at Woody's. He tells me about the glory holes in the bathroom of the New York Public Library. I tell him he's lying, that dogs aren't allowed in the library. I'm having trouble breathing. I sit down on the edge of the bed. I say, what, so women aren't good enough for you anymore! I remind him of our first date, how he tied me up and we cried all night. Never before had I been threatened with such tenderness, such sincerity. You can't fake that! I am yelling. I am not a woman if my dog doesn't want me.

I'm a question mark in a skirt. The dog has his sad puppy dog eyes on. I've seen him practice this look in the mirror. He asks me not to hate him. He rolls his eyes and whines.

I know that he's already picturing himself out on a walk, leaving me here alone in a room full of condoms and chew toys, some man's hand on his leash. I wonder if it's my scent that he finds so vile. He rests his chin on his crossed paws. It's not that you're fat, he tells me. There's a gland near the base of the skull that regulates it—this desire, this thing, for bones.

CHICKEN

Scott Pomfret

You were slouching under a blue sign that said "Bienvenue." Your platinum hair was tousled, your clothes-hanger hips showed above your belt, and you dangled your thumb as if you didn't give a shit in the world whether I picked you up.

You were fabulous. Exceptional. A wet dream. A should-not-stop. An orchid moment, to look at but not to touch. If I'd been smart, I'd have slammed the gas pedal and left you in my rear view, in the dust, middle finger extended and your eyes already returned to the road. You'd have been no more than a masturbatory fantasy and a pretty, idle sometime speculation that you could have been the one to make me happy.

But I spoiled it all. I stopped before I knew I'd stopped. You leaned in the window. Your dinner-plate eyes seized me, turned me upside down, then let me go. You took me for harmless, for all appearances a balding, placid fifty-three-year-old in a white Buick LeSabre my parents no longer had use for, along a two-lane highway three hours north of Portland, Maine, bound for Hell for all you cared, as long as I stopped at your hometown along the way.

Your handshake was the grip I hope to feel if ever I find myself dangling from the edge of the world. You talked enough for both of us. Your eyes misted over the roadkill we passed, and you wanted to know all the details of my parents' illnesses. You extolled the virtues of a good cry and the exquisite bitchiness of Courtney Love. You plucked the dried flower in my sun visor and flicked it out the window. You said belligerently, "When a thing isn't beautiful anymore, you should really throw it away." You fiddled with the radio dial and fished through your backpack for the new Cranberries album, which you said I absolutely had to hear. You were queeny and coy and confident and hot and generous and everything your looks promised you would be.

And you were only fifteen.

I knew it was wrong and impossible. I knew I should just let it go. There were people who counted on me after all, parents who cared, folks that would be disappointed, stricken, horrified. But your hand drifted to your belt, and sweat gathered in the depression between your collar bones, trembled, and then fell, drawing a neat wet line between your nipples, and these anonymous woods on either side of the highway gave me license.

We reached your hometown of Sabbaday far too soon. In the town square, a half-dozen boys with severe Caesar haircuts cooled us with insolent gazes. The prettiest boy—who was not even in your league—had bandanna'd his shirt around his head. He was idly shooting the breeze as he catalogued the heads that turned to check him out from passing cars. The sheriff, who was lounging in his patrol car beneath a faded billboard advertising Kools, glanced up as we passed and then returned to the dirty magazine open in his lap. There was an oddly canted, weathered sign in the square that pointed to distant towns all over the globe as if they were at an impossible remove.

"I hate this place," you said quietly. You were not bitter. You were not just another ordinary, desperate teenaged faggot not sure what he really wanted, a precocious too-smart too-pretty fairy in a too-small town just noticing the radical disconnection between what was in your heart and what everyone around you said belonged there, a boy who had not quite accepted that he was gay, or who did not really believe he was beautiful, or who harbored suspicion that inside himself there were all kinds of ugliness that no one else could see, and that, if seen, would keep anyone from loving him.

No, you were different. Your beauty required something greater of you. Aspirations. It required you, on behalf of the ugly and lazy and stupid of Sabbaday, to get out and make something of yourself, to piss on your family and neighbors and those you left behind.

They would not mind. They would understand. They would say: "See, he came from here, I knew him way back when. Everything is possible, so disconnect the garden hose from the exhaust pipe, pull it from the cracked front window, and live another day."

It was obvious, therefore, that you needed me to help you. That's what I told myself. That's the excuse I used for hanging around.

You pointed at a little convenience store under the fir trees that sold bait and ice. You said, "You can drop me here."

You lingered a long moment in the open door. You seemed reluctant to surrender me. You thanked me for the ride and wondered if our paths would ever cross again, and you shyly suggested that maybe I had learned something important from you along the way.

When I showed up eight hours later, at the end of your shift, you had forgotten my name but you were delighted.

"Hey!" you said.

You were working behind the rotisserie, where a couple of dried-out brown chickens turned perpetually on spits. Your hands were nicked and bloody.

As you washed up, you chattered on about the dozen birds you had to hack to pieces each day. You demonstrated for me in the air on an imaginary specimen, saying, "I stick a knife up the dead bird's ass, and cut though the bones where its chest was. I pull off all the skin and fat, snap the bones and drop them in the garbage. Hey . . . Can you give me a ride home?"

I took a room at a dirty motel where they made me pay a deposit for the sheets. All night, my greedy thoughts ransacked your sculpted chest, your smooth flat belly, the piano-key ribs beneath your armpits, the downy hair on your forearms, the blush in your cheek, the unmatched dimple that produced a wry expression when you smiled, the runaway eyes, the tousle of ragged hair, the dime nipples, the blue vein in your biceps, the delicate neck, the perfect ears with matched silver hoops, the little streak of dirt on the tip of your nose, and the self-conscious return your finger made to the one lock of hair that dangled over your forehead. My mind filled also with what I would never see: the neat tangle of pubic hair, arc of penis, the mound of ass on which your pants were slung, the athletic thighs and muscled calves and perfect ankles, all smooth and new and clean and young. I imagined what it would have been like to be fucked by you. To run greedy hands over you. To be loved by you.

I persuaded myself that if I had just this one moment of evergreen, this one brief exposure to pure beauty, I would be the happiest man in the world. And it was worth the chance of getting caught. Worth the shame. Worth defying the pieties of the age, the standard aversions issued in lily-white painted houses on cookie-cutter blocks in faceless towns, that say a boy like you could not love me.

It had been so long since I had held a man's hand. So long since I returned a look. I lived in my parents' house that was no longer a home. I went to bars that were no longer hospitable to my age. I stood around the Gay Studies section of the Barnes & Noble and hoped to see what the young boys were reading—but it was always with restraint, always look-and-no-touch, masking agitation with an air of perfect contentment, the placid acceptance of a child, to whom everything is new and strange, and therefore, for lack of experience, normal and endurable: No, ma, it does not bother me to change your diaper; no, what bothers me is that someday soon there'll be no one to need me.

And I convinced myself that, after all, I was not running away from a home anymore, not running from parents whose bodies were broken and minds were shells, not running from the fog hollows in my soul; no, I was running to. Running to you. To this god-forsaken little town called Sabbaday. I had stopped for you, so I told myself I was meant to stop. I told myself that I was doing you a favor. I would be good for you.

I am not a bad person. I struggle to be honest and true, to match word and deed, thought and conduct, ideals and executions. But over time a strange gulf has grown between the surface and what lies beneath. I get old and there's still a boy inside. I age, but still think of myself as beautiful. My parents become feeble, but still I think they invented fire.

The next day, when I arrived at the store, you were studying your face in a plastic compact you had retrieved from the trash.

"Look at this!" you demanded. "Just look. It's enormous!"

"What are you talking about?"

"The zit, man! The zit. What else?"

I reached out to pop a tiny blackhead, and you shrieked.

"Don't touch! It'll scar!" You held your hand protectively over your face like a woman in Purdah. "You just don't understand. For someone like you, it's not such a big deal, but because I'm so beautiful, a zit really means something to me . . . "

You stopped to consider that your words had not come out sounding very nice.

"Think of it," you added, almost defiantly, "would you have picked me up at the side of the road if I hadn't looked so good?"

"Yes," I lied.

"Do you think you could ever fall in love with me if I got ugly?"

My heart nearly stopped. "Sure," I agreed.

For a long moment, you held my gaze. A desperate voice spoke to me from some guttural region beneath your beautiful face: Take what you want of my body, the voice promised, and I'll trade it all for an ear. You were obviously willing to settle for that exchange, perhaps to call it love. I thought: We could be perfect together.

You returned to your reflection in the compact and decided, "If that happened, I'd kill myself. I mean, if I got ugly. Not if you fell in love with me. You know what I mean?"

I nodded. You looked relieved, and the proprietor, a heavy-set old man who sat on a stool behind the counter, nodded his silent approval.

"So where do you live, anyhow?" you asked, as you bagged another customer's groceries. "I thought I knew everyone around here."

"Boston," I admitted, jealous of even that small attention you would give someone else.

"Is that near here?"

"Boston, Mass. I'm a Masshole."

You laughed. "Duh," you said. "Stupid question. As if."

"No, really."

You froze. I slid my driver's license across the counter, and you snatched it up as if it were cheese in a trap. Your eyes flickered over it like a tongue and then returned to me, and all around us the color of the air changed abruptly.

"You better leave," you suggested, flipping the license to the counter and glancing around for the old man. For once, he was not there.

"You better leave," you said again. But you could not bring yourself to forbid me ever to come back again. None of us really want to risk that, for fear we will be someday left alone.

It took a bit of persuasion, but you agreed to walk, to talk, to let me buy you an ice cream, to explain myself. The boys hollered at you as we walked through the square. Your face turned hard as porcelain.

You ejaculated, "They're white trash! They used to harass me."

"White trash?" The words startled me. They had a vintage flavor, like a butter churn or cat eyeglasses. Where I am from, nobody uses them any more.

"My Mom got after them. She got the sheriff to arrest them for sexual harassment. My Mom protects me." You let that idea linger and then added threateningly, "and she sleeps with the sheriff, so she can make it stick."

"You don't have to threaten me, you know. Because I would never hurt you. In fact, I want to help you."

I ordered a cup of water at the ice cream shop and you sucked your straw and lined up the cherry on your sundae as if you would flick it into my eye.

You demanded, "Why would you lie? Did you think you had a chance with me?"

I said nothing.

"What about your parents? Were you lying about that, too?"

"No. They're being taken care of. We have insurance . . . There's a nurse."

"You don't ever see them?"

"I can't bear to."

Your eyes drank that in. Impossibly, you seemed to understand. For someone so young, you had such a great big understanding.

You remarked, "I'm never going to be old as them. I'm going to die young."

"Jesus, I hope not."

"What d'you care?"

"The world would be an emptier place if you weren't in it."

You were grateful I said that. You were tempted to believe me.

"You don't even know me," you snapped.

"I do know you! Don't tell me what I know and don't know!"

I leaned toward you over the table, tipping my cup of water and upsetting the napkin holder and pinning the table frame against your belly. Too much, too soon. You shrank at the table until you were a child hiding in an attic from his raging father. Terrified of being found. Terrified of not being found. Your little chest heaving, your fist blocking your mouth to keep from crying out, your heart battering your ribs. It continued to astonish me, this crazy plasticity of yours—one moment defiant and angry, the next terrified, the next unbearably sweet.

"What I mean," I amended gently, "is that I do know you. I do. On a level that defies words." In the window next to us, a bird's egg had fallen from the nest and cracked open on the black sill. The half-formed bird had spilled out and been cooked to the hot surface.

You examined my face with a look like frostbite. You patiently listed for me the reasons that you were a piece of shit. And why I should hate you. At eleven, you said, you had already begun to have thoughts of having sex with men, so you thought at first that your stepfather's raping you was a punishment from God.

You examined my face for reaction, perhaps even to see whether I believed you. When you were fourteen, you continued, you had smoked a hundred unfiltered cigarettes to try to make your voice more manly. But when you recorded it on tape, you found nothing had changed. And you labored for hours over your suicide note, draft after draft, to make sure that your mother never doubted that you loved her, and the white trash never took it into their heads that they had forced you to do this. You did it of your own free will.

Again you examined my face. You repeated this process, alternating confession and examination, until the sundae was gone, and there was only a slick of ice cream in the bottom of the dish and you had succeeded in souring my belly.

"I'm a mess," you complained. You rattled your spoon in the sundae dish and mumbled, "I should stop before you hate me."

"I'll never hate you."

"Yes, you will. Everybody does. I'm a bad, horrible person."

You ached for me to disagree.

And it might have turned out all right. It might have been that I had dredged up just the right salve for that particular split second of time, and we might have been friends forever and ever.

But then a tired mother opened the door to the ice cream parlor and spilled her brood inside. The mother's kids stared at us, bumping into one another at the short stop, like a line of boxcars in a rail yard.

You shouted, "What are you looking at, trash?!"

Then you looked at me, full of blame for having attracted the kids' attention. As if we were freaks or lepers, as if they saw all the way through us and knew our worst secrets, and our gayness, and the ugliness of what I wanted from you, a boy almost forty years younger.

"I have a boyfriend," you said.

My heart slow-burned into feathered ash. You were not innocent.

You described this thirty-eight-year old Portland chickenhawk whom you saw on weekends and said you loved. You said he was a DJ and promoted all the raves in Portland. You said he was a body builder, tall, tanned, and perfect, with a young man's hair and a nine-inch cock. You said he bought you shiny club clothes and kept your backpack loaded with CDs and all you had to do was fuck him once in a while, so what difference did it make that he had been married once and had a kid your age?

You got uglier every time I blinked. You were turning out to be one more lie, one more promise never fulfilled, one more dime-a-dozen platinum tease with a hard cock, narrow hips and pouting lips, but not a hint of courage. You were a chicken. You had already—at age fifteen—given up, and you were terrified to let me love you, afraid to let me lift you from this Sabbaday misery and show you something better. You talked a big game, you pretended you didn't give a rat's ass, you dared the shit to rain down on you, but deep down you believed you deserved it.

That was why— after I let you go back to work—you got all those guys from Sabbaday to confront me in the parking lot of that filthy little motel. They fled only when the Indian proprietor came running out clutching his fat little belly and singsonging some warning about the sheriff, and they warned me I should never come back.

You pretended you didn't know anything about the attack. You pretended you did not arrange it.

Spare me the bullshit. I pissed blood the whole next day.

So maybe it's true that you are, after all, just another dime-a-dozen platinum twit holding a permanent pity party in a back-woods trailer park. Maybe my ambitions for you were way too high. You were born white trash, and there's no compromising who you are.

But I could not allow you to think that I was like all the rest. That I had wanted nothing more than what was in your pants. I am a better person than that.

And admit it: You didn't want it to end that way, any more than me. You weren't immune to the what-happens-next. You wanted to read the story of your life.

And there's no shame in that. We all need a witness, no matter how frightening the story he tells. We all wish to be known, through and through, top to bottom, inside and out. If only to one person. If only for the briefest of moments. Which is maybe all any of us can hope to achieve, just a moment of witness that we can call love.

I dropped by the bait shop, and said, "If you've got nothing to do after work, why don't we hang out?"

You could easily have summoned your parking lot posse and told me to go to hell. But you said nothing. You fiddled with the knives at the carve station, and you pushed meat around the gleaming cutting board with a long-handled knife, and you set out three red-checked wax-paper rafts to serve the chicken breasts to a group of friends you did not have.

"It doesn't have to be tonight," I pointed out. "It could be . . ."

"Sure," you interrupted, "I guess we can hang out. After work."

"No sex," I promised. "That's not what I want."

"After work," you repeated.

"Really, it's not like that."

Your face remained as blank and firm as a tuber baking in the incubator flush of rotisserie light. You shot a glance at the old man on his stool on the other side of the room.

"Dude . . ." you said, "I gotta work."

When the old man locked up behind you, you seemed surprised that I'd dared to come. Your eyes passed over the DKNY shirt. The Gucci shoes. You saw I had gotten all dressed up for the occasion, and you said sullenly, "Your shirt's hanging out."

Crestfallen, I asked, "What would you like to do?"

"I don't know. This was your idea."

"What do you normally do in Sabbaday?"

"Hang out."

We went back to my motel room. The bed was covered with raspy sheets you insisted were stained with cum. You threw yourself on it. You were so small and dark against that king-sized white spread that you looked like a teddy bear that belonged to a lonely child, clutched and worn and mistakenly left behind.

"At least," you said, "It's got HBO."

All night long, from a chair on the far side of the room, I watched your unquiet sleep. Just after midnight, you bolted upright in bed, loosed a stillborn cry, and then again fell flaccid among the covers.

I thought: I am trying to do too much. You will never be happy.

But morning proved me wrong. You woke like your old self, restored, beautiful as I had ever imagined you, and cheerful and charming and kind, and maybe even slightly grateful that I had not tried anything on you in the night. You rested your ass half on the windowsill, colt legs splayed out in front of you, the loose tongue of your leather belt flopped sideways.

You chattered up a storm, you called your mother to check in. As you lied to your mother about where you had been, you shot me a demanding, conspiratorial, entertain-me-now look.

Something vast, unnameable, and pure swelled inside me. I dared to believe that I still might win from you some small redemption, short of what I had dreamed, but better by far than nothing.

"Come on," I said, "you definitely need to get out of here. Come with me."

Wariness and hope and open-mouthed curiosity raced one another over your face.

"Where to?"

I honestly did not know. Somewhere. Anywhere. Faraway. High. Worthy. Sage. My mind spun like a slot machine, and then—jackpot! Three cherries in a row.

"Do you hike?" I asked.

"Sure . . ."

"Show me a trail."

The sun seemed loud and companionable, birds soared, rambunctious chipmunks scattered the path ahead. The beech trees had turned yellow and rustled in the new breeze, like dogs shaking off a skin of water.

I could not wound you that day. Could not touch you. You scampered off into the woods and hid at the bend of the trail and then jumped out at me. Your eyes were so bright, everywhere you looked was in danger of forest fire.

We reached the summit in late afternoon. It was an exposed patch of boulders and flat rock just above treeline and it felt like no one but you and me had ever been there before. I pointed to the south, toward Boston.

"Look! If you squint, if you look as far as you can hope to see, you can see it, can't you? The glint of it under the haze?"

You raised a hand to your eyes, you looked where I looked. You did not deny it.

I was overjoyed. There was hope for you yet. Maybe you wouldn't conquer the world, maybe you would not even get out of Sabbaday, but there were hills to climb and more modest successes, and there was in you still a hint of courage and still in me enough virtue to get us by.

I sat back against a worn boulder, arms hugging my aching knees, and gazed over the valley. You flopped down full length on the flat rock, your eyes at half-mast, staring up at the sky.

I tried to contain myself, to stifle my own breaths. To be nothing more than the warmth and love and happiness that had long eluded you. To be humor, solace, nurture, and forgiveness, the pure and physical manifestation of all these things, so that you would know that you were not alone, or if alone, that you could be comforted. That was all I was shooting for, no more, and I wanted to say: You don't have to love me, boy, but somewhere, you will find love. It will all be good.

But you couldn't be content with that. You couldn't compromise. Even as the sun began to set, you jumped up and yanked off your shirt. You threw it to the side, where it fell open on the flat rock like a body chalked on the sidewalk.

You stretched and preened and turned like meat on spit under the late afternoon's oven-red light. You ran your hands over your body, until there seemed to be a hundred hands, hands all over you, on your shoulder, your nipple, your rippled belly, your tug-taut crotch. Shadow played over one side of your body, and fading sunlight over the other, and even your breaths seemed like yet another hand on your skin.

You took a keen interest in my interest in you. You searched my face. You crooked your head like a faithful dog.

"Tell me how pretty I am," you said.

You drew the scars on your wrists with your finger, flexed your hip, scratched your belly.

You asked, "Ya wanna know why I fuck around?"

"No, but . . ."

"Me and my friend Darcy made a bet that whoever fucks the most people by the time they're eighteen gets . . ."

"Hey!" I barked. The sound echoed in the deep of the valley, and then came back to us.

"Yeah?"

"Shut your pie hole. You don't have to show off for me."

A flame flared over your face, and then resolved into bruised granite. Heat shrank from the ember-red sky and followed the sun behind the hills.

"You're a better person than that," I persisted.

You said, "We should go. It's going to get dark."

You were looking off through the clearing toward the valley below, toward Sabbaday, and clutching your shirt in your hands.

You said, "I don't even know why I came."

I rocked forward from where I was sitting to a low crouch at your feet, as if I could block your escape. My head was at the level of your crotch. You were angled slightly away from me.

I said, "You don't have to be white tra—"

"There was this party I was thinking of going to. Now, because of you, I'm going to miss it . . ."

Your voice trailed off, and even though my eyes were on your crotch, I knew you must have looked down on me. At the sun spots on my scalp. The round shoulders. Gray hair. Your revulsion was palpable as the hard stone under my knees or the growing cold in my joints. My heart dropped like an elevator. Nobody had ever made me feel as ugly as you did then. You put me in a whole new class of old and undesirable, a stinking place of ear hair and jealousy and trench coats and flecks of white spittle on old rubber lips.

I mumbled, "Sorry to have wasted your time. I know it's true, I am not as handsome as you had hoped."

An exasperated noise issued from the back of your throat, and you gave an electric, impatient start that realigned your hips, so they were head on, square to my face, a perfect alignment of planets, and I knew suddenly that this was exactly how it had always been fated to be.

"I don't mean it like that," you pleaded. Your ab muscles wrestled as you spoke. "I like you."

"No, you're absolutely right. Absolutely. We should go. We should leave this place." I did not move. I stayed crouched at your crotch, until I felt forced to explain: "It's just . . . I've been where you are now . . . . I feel a sense of, of, of destiny, a sense of obligation to you."

Your voice was like the rattle of pennies in a jar: "Wow," you said. "And you haven't even fucked me yet . . ."

"I'm not going to fuck you."

"Whatever you need to tell yourself."

You stepped around me and walked stiffly toward the edge of the clearing to the trail.

I called out, "What do you like about me? What exactly?"

You froze in your tracks before you had reached the safety of the trees.

"You know what?" you said. "I lied. I don't like you."

For a second, the world did not turn, and my heart blew out like a birthday candle. Then, your fixed expression dissolved into champagne laughter, and you struck out giggling down the trail, hurtling through open branches, heedless of the stones underfoot.

I leapt up and chased you, colliding at a bend in trail where you had stopped, swallowed by the anonymous shadow of a hemlock tree.

You seized me to keep from getting bowled over. In my ear, your voice was a rasp, arch, urgent, all throat, and vaguely threatening: "Here," you said, "you want to, you can do it here. In the dark. If you want to. I won't tell."

Your eyes were dark and ringed. Your breath was hot. A single sprig of hemlock hung over your face like mistletoe.

"Come on," you hissed. You clutched at my hand and drew it to your waist, and your belly was warm as the fresh bread my mother once used to make.

I could not help myself. I forced myself on you. I drove you back against the tree with all the strength left in this fat old body.

You gasped as a branch pierced your backside. But you didn't struggle. You didn't stop me. You were mannequin stiff, feet rooted firmly in the needle bed, and you fixed your gaze over my shoulder at some unfathomable distance, so that—even though I held you in my own two hands—it felt as if I had lunged and missed.

There was not a whisper of wind. Not a witness in the world. No one was watching.

I sank to my knees. I clung to your belt. You were not there, I swear, it was just an abandoned body, a hollowed chest. You did not see me close my eyes, you did not see me part my lips. You did not see me at all, this old man kneeling, giving head to the hard kindling of the old hemlock tree until his mouth was cut and gummed with sap, and the bark stripped and bleeding, and broken branches pointed every which way.

THE PARAPHILIA ODES

Steven Burt

1

O my companions in microfiber & leather
O my companions in spangle & tulle
O my companions cat carriers in hand
Great treasure has been given to you to lose

2   [to W. 125th St.]

High subway rails stretch out and out like fraud. The suave
horizon never stops.
Their calculations mount. A surly
Witness, you know what confronts you; none of your
Wishing suffices to push the facts away.
You would have done better to stay where you were, she said;
Now you will never know where you are.

3

Nothing holy is real.
Renunciation is the new appeal.
Our memories don ratty water wings
And slap and flail their way across our pond.
At thirteen we learned to hide in their closets and listen
As if we could learn from the latest, the most secret noise.
Who did we love? Not the ones who returned our first calls:
By the end of each year we had to prove ourselves
Again. We never did. This poem, like all poems,
Takes place entirely in school. It has

Left the sensuous details entirely for the next section
Which cannot assemble them, not even with you.

4 [tenth grade]

He follows the tiny bones
At the beloved's wrist,
Their workings as she writes on posterboard.
Candycane polish flakes from one toenail.
The alluvial fan of the bones at the top of the foot
Slides inwards as his bare toe touches hers.
She has cut off the collar from her Izod shirt
So that it exposes her clavicle, then falls straight
Along her ribs. He feels them when they kiss.
It is the deviations from the script
Of her body and his, the absences and
Mistakes, that excite him most:

The sweat that darkens the crotch
Of her flat, plaid, red-on-green
Underpants whose cotton has worn smooth,
The slack elastic at the waist, through which,
All too gingerly, she leads his palm.
The two of them stop
There. He will always stop there.
He will ask his future lovers for nothing else,

And nothing more, and nothing less.

5

The Fall is not the discovery of sin but the discovery of responsibilities, consequences, open-ended or indefinite obligations: the mere
knowledge of good and evil is itself the end of a kind of joy, since
we are so made as to let that knowledge guide us, or at least to pretend that it does, to strive for at least the appearance of favoring
others' pleasure over our own. (Eve did not give up anything for
Adam before the discovery of the apple, nor did he ever ask that she
do so.) As we grow we "fall" deeper, accumulating, and remembering, ever more obligations; we therefore see people younger than we
are (rightly or wrongly) as lacking them, and long for the faraway

time in our own lives when we believe we could have acted selfishly without knowing that acting selfishly was wrong. We therefore
encourage our friends and partners, as adults, to become or remain
more childlike than we believe ourselves to be, not only because we
can guide them (and participate vicariously in their pleasures) but
because we feel guilty for our own desires in a way that we do not
for theirs—in the imagined economy of Eros, ambition, assistance,
and self-denial, their desires do not necessarily interfere with our
obligations. And so we take greater pleasure, for much of our lives,
in helping our friends or partners get what they want than we do in
taking what we want for ourselves.

6   [for an AB]

Barely aware how I melt * artifice and warm
Light * let me lie with * this secret don't make me
Tell * everything feels slippery * where I can't
Speak * only cry * your mattress held me
Up * from the balls of my feet * rough plastic
Clings around my hips * keeping safe
My nightly diaper * softening where I am
Held * have I wet * the bed * am I
Asleep * if I wake * the caudal bone
Still wet * where I wet myself * between my
Legs some part lost * the rest * wash me
Away let me fall * on my
Bare knees * dress me * up as your tiny
Possession * change me * make me nothing now

7   [for Christmas Eve]

Fake fish outside the sex toy store (inside
Its story-high front window) swim around
On strings, on strings; their pulleys rise indoors
To circle in midair, on a blue scrim
Lit up to look like water—corals, moss,
A diver's rusty effigy. Inside,
Fluorescence says, we shop below the waves—
The fuschia, pea-green, and ultramarine
Subsurfaces and trenches of desire . . .

What could these scarlet thigh-highs do, equipped
As each one is, with batteries and lights?
Who would these leather socks and kerchiefs please?
The laws of natural history are exact
As laws of pleasure: just this, nothing else,
No other fabric, chain or term of art
Controls the night or makes observers grin.
From their evolved mosaic underground
At 81st Street Station, trilobite
And Gila monster, shark and bowerbird
Stare out to where cold passengers meet trains:
Weighed down with bright-eyed shopping, our sex toys
Still heavy in our bags, we disembark
To meet the eyes of creatures who meets ours
As if to ask us: How do you get off?

CONFESSIONS OF A DIAL-UP GIGOLO

Neal Pollack

A guy can't choose when he comes of romantic age. It happened for me in 1993, when the telltale buzz and "ping-ping-ping" modem sound really started to fill the air in the middle-class American home. That was the summer that everyone fell in love at the keyboard. I found myself addicted to chat rooms' thin but fresh charms.

My 1980s high school liaisons in the backs of vans seem closer now than the dozens, if not hundreds, of hours I spent staring at the grayish-blue screen of my Mac Classic, bopping from room to room, looking for an invitation to "go private." At the beginning, you could sign on to AOL and expect to see the same basic group of people in the same basic place. As little as two years later, someone could introduce themselves with the charming words, "I Will Cum 4 U." But in the early days, old-fashioned, seductive conversation was still possible.

Early one evening, I signed on and went to my usual spot, which was called something like "Book Chat" or "Smart People Seek Smart People." There, waiting, sat "Googol." I checked the profile. It appeared to be a woman, and her profile mentioned something about being "infinitely wise." Well, I thought, I'm always looking for one of those.

Googol and I got involved in the group chat. After about an hour, we'd determined that everyone else in the room was hopelessly stupid. After two hours, she sent me an Instant Message.

"Wanna go back to my place?" she wrote.

"Sure," I said.

She set up a private chat room. The next three hours were a tease and a dodge. I told her secrets I didn't know I had and she poured open her soul to me. She was in her late forties and lived in a suburb of Boston. Her husband was a pharmacist who had long ago given up on life. They had a teenage daughter who suffered from lupus. Right there, that fact should have stopped me. This was an adult woman with very adult problems. What did I have? I lived in a semi-communal apartment with some urban hippies. I wanted to be a writer. And I was worried that the director of ImprovOlympic wasn't going to put me on the right "team." Googol and I made a bad match.

People who haven't had an online affair mock those of us who have. But at the time, the connections feel every bit as intense and tender, and the sex every bit as good as what happens in the physical world. The breakups are also just as spectacular and sad. From the beginning, I might as well have been trying to prevent a train crash. Googol and I were bonded.

Eventually, we started talking on the phone, but we didn't have phone sex because her husband was always home.

"He knows all about you," she said. "All about my friend Neal, who lives in Chicago. I didn't tell him about the other stuff."

That Boston pharmacist must have really been numb to the world, because when your partner starts talking about their "special friend," it's a sure sign that they're conducting an affair. The evenings melded together. Googol and I talked for an hour or two. Then we'd hang up the phone, go online, and masturbate together. Sometimes, when we were done, we'd talk again.

She was completely unhinged, in a quiet way. The tip-off should have been the story about the symphony violinist she'd met in the Boston subway who told her she was beautiful, and subsequently pursued her until she succumbed to a night of passion. Then he wrote a concerto for her, and committed suicide. At the time, it all seemed perfectly plausible to me, but a decade's perspective allows me to see that the story was a total lie, a kind of romance-novel fantasy for the NPR set. Why hadn't the guy been a violinist and a novelist, or, even better, a poet?

"You're incredible," I said. "I want to see what you look like."

She sent me a photograph taken twenty years earlier. It might as well have been Ali McGraw from *Love Story*. The soulful brown eyes, the lustrous black hair, the knee drawn up to the chin, the look that said, "I did really well in my grad school Byron seminar. Wanna smoke a joint and fuck?" The photo was all that made me really long for the seventies.

"I've never seen someone so beautiful," I said.

"That woman is gone," she said. "But the eyes. I still have the eyes."

I knew my relationship with Googol was in trouble the night she IM'ed me the following phrase: "Have you heard of the book *The English Patient?*"As a reminder of how long ago this occurred, it was before the movie that didn't deserve its Oscar.

"I have heard of it," I said. "It's not supposed to be very good."

That was a lie, but I was trying to head pretension off at the pass.

"Steve told me I had to read it," she said.

"Steve" had started to come up a lot. I'd been a little busier than usual and was not as attentive online as at the dawn of our love. Steve stayed online all the time. He lived in Chicago, too, Googol said. Wasn't that something? He worked as an executive at Quaker Oats, and he was divorced, and he wrote the most beautiful poetry.

This need not be dragged out. Googol left me for Steve. She was also leaving her husband for Steve. This would all happen at the end of the summer, after she'd gathered the courage to tell her husband that she was leaving him. She told me all this over the phone.

"But you know I'll always have a special place in my heart for you, Neal," she said.

By that point, I had girlfriends in the real world and I was pretty sick of this pretentious nobody. But all the sex and fancy talk had muddled me.

"And I, you," I said to Mrs. Robinson.

"I've told Steve all about you," she said. "He really wants to meet you."

For some reason, I agreed. So on a lovely late-summer afternoon, I met Steve at a bad outdoor restaurant on the north bank of the Chicago River. My memory is faded. But I think he had blond curly hair going gray and a soft but somewhat beaten face.

"She speaks very highly of you," he said.

"Thanks," I said. "I saw a picture of her. She used to be really hot."

I had just said that to a stranger about the woman who he was probably going to marry. He looked at me like I was vermin. I wanted to say, "Hey, old man, fuck your midlife crisis. I loosened her up for you." But instead, we talked for a while about how I wanted to write a novel, and then he paid the bill and Googol was no more.

Three years later, distraught by the end of a bad physical-world relationship that had gone on far too long, I returned to the chat rooms. By then, the AOL air, while still not the perversion circus it became at its height, was much less rarified. My old haunts were crowded with dudes trolling for babes. The exclusive filter had disappeared.

Somehow, I found Jojo, who also lived in Boston. She was a language therapist who worked with troubled children, believed in a clean environment, was a total succubus, and just wasn't getting what she wanted from her husband, Kevin. Naturally, we had chatroom sex on the night we met.

Within a week, we were on the phone every night, because Kevin worked nights. When he was home at night, Jojo called me during the day while he took a nap. She concocted errands so she could leave the house and call me on her cell phone. Why? Because we were having explosive multi-orgasmic masturbation sessions.

"No one makes me come like you do!" she said.

"I love you!" I said.

"I love you, too!"

"I love, love, love, love, love you! Oh God! Now! Now! Now! Uhhhh!"

It proceeded along this subtle path for a month or so. One night, Jojo was driving home from a dinner party. She and Kevin had taken separate cars. I got a phone call. Within seconds, she was masturbating furiously with one hand, while driving with the other.

"Oh, Neal!" she said. "You're mine! You're mine forever!"

"Yes, Jojo, yes!" I said.

"I'm leaving Kevin," she said.

"Good call!" I said.

Two weeks went by with no contact as Jojo's life collapsed around her. I went out on a couple of dates, one of them with the woman who I would later marry. When Jojo next checked in with me, she had news. First, Kevin moved out. Second, she moved out herself and had found her own apartment. Third, she met a nurse at a party. Fourth, the nurse moved in with her. Fifth, they purchased a puppy. Sixth, they went on vacation to the Cape. Seventh, she was now a lesbian.

"Wow," I said. "Those are some pretty big changes."

"Thanks for helping me realize my true self," she said.

"Oh, no problem," I said.

A few weeks later, I was seized by a fit of midnight jealousy. We had a screaming fight. The tender friendship that had built up in the aftermath of Jojo's conversion to the other side blew apart. She kept me on her email list for a couple of years, mostly updates about redecorating the apartment or pleas for money from the Sierra Club. My soon-to-be-wife and I visited Boston. I planned to see Jojo, who was laid up with a broken leg, but my soon-to-be-wife wasn't so into that idea. Then I blocked her from my friends list and she, too, was gone forever.

So there we are. Two marriages in Boston ended, at least partially with my help, without me ever meeting any of the parties involved except for that Steve fellow. Several lives were forever altered by my actions and words, but mine remained essentially the same. It turns out I was looking for the same level of intimacy you get with someone who you get along with on the airplane, but with masturbation added. My "lovers," on the other hand, were looking to utterly transform themselves. This didn't bring me satisfaction, or sadness, or any kind of feeling, really. After all, I didn't even know them.

THE ART OF REBOUND

Phil West

You realize you are already packing too quickly,
forgetting the toothpaste and comb,
too hasty with the zipper. You will arrive at her door,

the unexpected guest, roses in your arms.
You're thinking fairy tale. Although it's obvious
you are oh so ready to be the one

crawling into bed, donning the bonnet
to wait for the basket brought up to you
by innocent hands, you're thinking fairy tale.

Prince at the edge of the bed, the kiss,
the gratitude, castles, the wedding dress
with a plunging neckline. You've got it scripted,

fish and red wine, so hopelessly mismatched.
Your heart thinks itself an empty stomach,
forgets its diet, wants a taste. You have done

the deep breathing, practiced your hello,
you move from hello how are you
to the very core of it, how very Eve's apple

it was when you first met. You have every right
to be thinking swagger and the sure opening line,
the red pen correcting the past, the happy ending.

But she is spoken for. She keeps

a prince on retainer, and there you are,
slighter as you slip through,

dropping from the stage lights above
to the couch of tender care. She's got
a notebook, glasses on the bridge of her nose,

you look up, and you are in the tired tableau
again, speaking it into the ceiling. And all you want
is a relocation program for the heart

as she speaks it back to you:
the sweets and the nothings,
the voice of the loved.

CHANGE THE WORLD

Cris Mazza

1986

It was around then Home Depot opened less than a mile away. It was the first one Marcy had seen. Someday it would be torn down because it was too small. But back then, it was the most enormous hardware store anyone had ever imagined. Bigger than Handyman, than Builder's Emporium, than Dixieline Lumber. It went in where an old FedMart had been standing empty, so not everyone was worrying about big box stores' accelerating sprawl, although Marcy voted for the no-development city councilmen.

After being married five years, Marcy and Kurt had bought a house. By changing little things in their lives and routine, they'd been able to save the down payment. She prepared meals from raw, fresh ingredients, and packed Kurt's lunch—cream cheese, walnuts, and sprouts, or cheese, lettuce, and tomato sandwiches—instead of him going out. She repainted the furniture she had in her apartment, the same stuff her mother had gotten from the Salvation Army thirty years ago. She and Kurt shared the 1979 sub-compact car Marcy had bought in the first year after graduating high school, and she put all of her bank teller salary into a money market account, then just paid the bills with Kurt's paycheck. To stretch his salary, they seldom went out to a concert or movie, never went on vacations, hadn't even had a honeymoon except African nut soup at The Prophet, their favorite vegetarian restaurant—decorated with portraits of Mohammed, Confucius, the Dali Lama, the Maharishi, Rama, Lord Vishnu, even Jesus.

Their real estate agent had complained once that a client had looked too long at her legs instead of at the houses she was showing. Marcy giggled about that later to Kurt, because the woman had chalky-white legs the size of baseball bats. Still snickering, Marcy had speculated aloud whether the woman's sexy legs would help her make sales. Kurt merely suggested,"Maybe she knows how to use them." After closing escrow, the agent gave them a gift coupon from a home-improvement catalogue. Marcy said, "At least she's not offering you her legs," and chose a socket wrench set. Her father had never gone anywhere without his, and an extra one had always sat open on the coffee table.

On one side of their new house, the neighbor had a pile of rocks just about filling her backyard. The houses were built with their backyards against a little hill made of sandstone with smooth, globular rocks mixed in, as though this was close to the river, which it wasn't. Some freak of geology caused the hill to continually spill into the neighbor's backyard. Marcy planned to put iceplant groundcover on the embankment above her yard. Their piece of the hill wasn't falling, but it was bare, with hardened gullies of erosion.

The other neighbor had weedy grass a foot high, shaggy oleander bushes growing through a rusty chain link fence adjacent to Marcy's driveway, and a cinderblock wall separating the two backyards. But their street ran downhill, so that neighbor's backyard was higher than Marcy's, and the cinderblock wall that was over Marcy's head in her yard only came up to her neighbor's waist in his (just as the wall on the other side of the yard only came to Marcy's waist and she could look down into the yard full of rocks). The weedy-lawn neighbor also had a dog who put its front feet on the cinderblock wall and barked, with spit flying, every time Marcy went into her own backyard.

Kurt didn't notice these things because he didn't go into the yard. He practiced his Tai Chi and his electric keyboard and previewed promotional record albums inside the house. He was manager of a Wherehouse record store. So he was indoors the Saturday the police visited, after Marcy called them. Marcy had been in the yard trying to figure out what she should do about the places in the lawn that were just bare dirt because half the year they got no sun. (Sowing more seeds wouldn't do any good. She thought about some sort of raised garden bed where she could grow vegetables, with park-like benches mounted on the timbers enclosing the garden.) The neighbor with the dog was actually watering his scrubby grass and disheveled bushes. He was also smoking and tossed his butt into Marcy's yard. Marcy retrieved it and went to the wall, holding the cigarette up toward the man as though passing a smoke up to a prisoner in a second floor cell.

"Please don't toss trash into my yard. This is still smoldering, it could've caused a fire."

"What?" the man replied. It looked like he might have no teeth.

She held the butt even higher. "Don't throw your cigarettes into my yard!"

The man turned, and his hose turned and squirted Marcy in the face.

The police, who arrived alarmingly quickly, spoke to the man, then knocked on Marcy's door. Kurt had to turn down Miles Davis or Chuck Mangione, Marcy couldn't tell them apart, although she did her Jazzercise to one of them.

"I don't think there'll be any more trouble, ma'am. He says it was an accident."

"He tossed a burning cigarette into our yard."

"He's just an old alky," the other cop said. "We'll drive past a few times in the next half hour. He'll calm down."

"Alky?" she'd asked Kurt, after the police left.

"Alcoholic." He was cleaning the record with special solution and a dust-free cloth. "Didn't he remind you of anyone?"

"Not particularly."

"Your father?"

"My father's not an alcoholic."

"Well, you should've called the police on your father, not our new neighbor."

"You didn't do anything."

"Do what? About what? Your father? I didn't even know you then." Kurt didn't look at her, slipping the record into its sleeve.

"No, you could've gone out and said something to . . . the old alky."

"Say what? About what?"

"He squirted me with the hose. It was no accident."

"So stay away from him." He pulled another record out of the stacked wooden grocery crates that exactly fit record albums. "Leave the yard alone, leave the grass alone, leave the hill alone, don't try to teach the neighbor manners. Why are you always trying to change everything?"

"To make things better."

"Better than what? Why can't things just be what they are? Why can't you just move into a house and live in it?"

"You mean don't fix anything?"

"Who's saying it needs fixing? Broken things need fixing. Leave everything else alone."

Marcy decided to put up a fence against the cinderblocks that would be high enough to block the dog and his owner from looking into her yard. Ten-foot-high fence boards would do it. Nail the fence boards, side by side, to two parallel sixteen-foot two-by-fours—one two-by-four securing the fence boards at three feet from the bottom, the other two-by-four fastened three feet above that. Then stand the fence up flush against the cinderblock wall, and just pound six-foot metal stakes into the ground on the other side to keep the board fence upright. After that, she would undertake the raised vegetable garden surrounded by picnic benches.

Her father never hit her, never laid a hand on her. He also didn't drink, no more than anyone else. He went to work, came home. He drove a cement truck for a while. Then other kinds of trucks. Gravel trucks, trucks delivering dirt here, picking up dirt from there. The things trucks did. If she still knew him, he could help pick up and deliver the railroad ties she would use to make the raised garden bed. But the last time she'd seen him was the day she'd arrived home from junior high and found her clothes, her shoes, her stuffed animals, and caged rat all piled on the front lawn. Her dad had decided it was time for her to move in with her mother. If it hadn't happened, she wouldn't have met Kurt, because her mother lived a hundred miles away in Sacramento, with her new husband. It was too late to imagine her parents would ever get back together anyway, but someday her father surely would have to at least explain.

Kurt was three years older, a senior when Marcy started high school. He was in the band. Marcy was on the drill team that followed the band down the street, making crisp synchronized motions with white-gloved hands, the metal taps on the heels of their white boots clicking in unison. Their school mascot was a yellowjacket, so there wasn't much of a ready-made costume, except yellow and black. They'd worn tailored miniskirts, yellow with black inside the pleats. There was an alternate uniform that was black with yellow inside the pleats. But she hadn't really known Kurt then, just knew who he was because he was the band's president and marched with his trombone in the center of the front rank. She and Kurt didn't start dating until Marcy was a senior. Kurt came back for the homecoming football game. By then Marcy had quit her position as captain of the synchronized-hands marching unit and joined a boycott of the whole homecoming queen ritual. She was picketing outside the football stadium, carrying a sign that said Cow Auction Today and chanting "Hey-Hey, Ho-Ho, this big boob contest has got to go." Kurt was in a little group of former band members who tried to drown them out with Sousa marches.

Apparently sparrows lived inside the Home Depot, it was that big. They flitted and chirped in the metal rafters overhead. Marcy was looking up as she wheeled a clunky lumber cart that never had all four wheels on the ground at the same time. She'd already loaded twenty-four ten-foot by eight-inch cedar fence boards and the two eight-foot two-by-fours. As she was pausing at the bins of nails, adding in her head, an employee passed, directing a customer farther down the aisle toward metal screws and bolts. The customer was someone Marcy knew. It was Colin, a boy from high school. Not just any boy, but her boyfriend in the tenth and eleventh grades. She knew it was him even though this man was getting fat. His pants were too tight and he had a gut straining against a T-shirt over his overly western belt buckle. His face was wide, his nose was broad, his head was enormous. His hair was considerably shorter than in 1978, and the blue on his face where he shaved was only on his chin and upper lip. In high school, Colin had grown a fringe-like mustache, and Marcy had been glad when he'd had to shave it off for the two months of band competitions. He played the snare drum in marching band and timpani in the school orchestra, which replaced marching band as an elective in the spring. Colin had liked a girl who played cello as much as he liked Marcy, so he alternated between the two of them for two years, going with Marcy during band season and the cello girl during orchestra season. In eleventh grade, when the band and auxiliary marching units visited Disneyland after their last tournament of the year, Marcy had shoplifted a knit hat from a gift kiosk when Colin did; she thought if she didn't, it might be his excuse that year to break up with her so he could go with the cello player during orchestra season. At first, Marcy was only choosing one of the longshoremen's hats because Colin was getting one. Then when she turned toward the cash register, he'd said, "Are you going to pay for it?" He'd balled his hat in his fist and turned to walk away, so she'd followed. They'd gotten caught. A grim plainclothes security guard led them to an office down a concealed alley off Disneyland's main street where they sat opposite a desk from another man. The shoplifted hats rested on the desktop along with some of the other junk they'd actually bought, like some sort of stuffed lizard from the Tiki Hut. The lizard stood on his mangled wire-manipulated feet with his mouth open and teeth showing, facing Marcy, and she just stared back at it, tears gushing, Colin hunched beside her while the man reamed them and said he was calling their parents, but as far as Marcy knew he never did (unless he called her father by mistake). On the bus ride back to Sacramento, Colin and Marcy hadn't spoken. They'd sat crushed together in the back of the bus, Colin's hand in Marcy's shirt, rhythmically squeezing one breast, and Marcy wept every now and then because she knew he would break up with her for the cello girl anyway. And he had, after not seeing Marcy at all during Christmas break.

It's not that Marcy thought about Colin once a week, even once a month, hardly even once a year, in fact. But when she did, she had wondered if Colin would someday contact her and apologize for the shit he pulled in high school. Once when she'd mentioned that idea to Kurt, he'd laughed and said it would keep the post office and phone company in business indefinitely if everyone apologized to everyone they'd fucked over in high school. "Well, I would, if I'd jerked anyone around," Marcy had said.

"How about those girls trying to be homecoming queen?"

"My right to free speech."

"You threw mud on them."

"I did not!"

When he saw her, Colin said "Hi," but not a surprised haven't-seen-you-in-years Hi, just Hi. His smile didn't exactly exclude his eyes, but didn't include them either. Colin was half Japanese and his almond eyes could be vacant when he stared dispassionately— like the times he broke up with her, or the time she didn't want to try his mother's seaweed-wrapped rice rolls—but she thought they had squinted merrily when he smiled, although she couldn't remember a specific time.

Colin's pants were too tight for him to put his hand in his pocket. He wedged his fingers in up to his knuckles, shifted his weight to one leg. Marcy was wearing overalls. She thought she might've had them since high school, but she could be remembering her painter pants, which she'd worn at a few school events, like the Earth Day rally, at which they'd chanted, "All we are sayyyying . . . is give hemp a chance," and carried signs that said Hemp, not Trees. They'd also spread dirt over part of the quad, to protest the paving of America. She'd loaned the stuffed lizard from Disneyland to a boy who had a sign that said Ours to Protect, Not Destroy.

Colin was wearing his inscrutable mask, the same face he wore the time he'd been absent from school on December 7th. When he came back the next day some boys started calling him Tojo. It was probably near the time Colin would be breaking up with Marcy after band season, so she hadn't said anything back to the kids who were ragging on him.

"So . . . you building a . . ." Colin examined her lumber cart, " . . . paneling a room?"

"No, just a fence. A piece of a fence. Long story. I live near here, do you?"

"I moved to San Jose. But I own a rental house in Alta Valley. Needs some rain gutters."

"Wow, you own an extra house? It would've been weird if we'd ended up renting from you. We finally bought a house, Kurt and I. Kurt Carlson, remember him?"

"I don't know anyone from high school anymore."

"Me neither . . . except Kurt, I guess. I didn't know him then. But you would know that. Hey . . . whatever happened to, you know . . . she played in the orchestra . . . ?"

Colin's expression, which maybe she was learning to read again, waited for more information before he finally shrugged. And as though giving in to someone pestering for a life story, he said, "I met my wife at work. When I was a security guard. Then I finished my associate degree and got a real estate license. I have three kids."

"Already?"

He didn't smile. He also didn't ask if she had any, so maybe it was obvious she didn't. The Earth Club in high school had some Zero Population Growth literature, and she'd mailed in a postage-paid card joining a mass pledge not to have children. Before she got married, she'd been saving her money to get her tubes tied, but when she made the budget so they could save for a down payment, her savings all went into the house account. Not that it mattered that much anymore. Marcy and Kurt hadn't had sex in over a year. Sometimes she wondered if Kurt wondered what had happened to them, or what he thought about when he thought about it, or if he used Tai Chi to forget about it.

Colin cleared his throat, then said, "So . . . did you ever become a lawyer?"

"A lawyer?"

"Didn't you want to be a lawyer?"

"When?" she laughed, "before or after my life in petty crime?"

"You're kidding."

"No, you know . . . Disneyland . . .?

What was on his face . . . confusion? Marcy felt hot and looked up into the rafters. The sparrows were twittering contentedly. It had become part of the Home Depot white noise: forklifts beeping, paint-shaking machines ratcheting, shoppers droning, lumber carts groaning, squeaking, banging . . . sparrows singing. A bird paused on a box of deadbolt locks on the top shelf of the aisle, in its beak a few bristles, perhaps from a broom or a paintbrush.

"Nesting." As Marcy spoke, the sparrow fluttered higher, into the roof beams. "Like us. We were going to change the world."

Colin was watching her, not exactly staring, but as though she was growing an extra eye and that's exactly what she was supposed to do, and what he expected.

"Well . . . time to go make lunch for Kurt, or he might succumb to the smell of frying fat from the McDonald's on the corner. Want to come see my house and have a bite to eat?"

"No thanks. I've got some guys waiting to install gutters."

"Okay. You might not like radish sprout salad and miso bean soup anyway." She looked down at the box of nails she'd been holding all the while, remembering she only had peanut butter and cracked wheat bread at home.

Marcy had been a vegetarian since before going to live with her mother. Secretly at first, because her father still wanted beef or pork with every meal, and since fourth grade Marcy had cooked his dinners for him. But she'd taken a vow against meat when she was twelve, the day her father squashed her new kitten under his truck tries in the driveway then took the mashed carcass and fed it to his dog. Kurt had been skeptical about the vegetarian diet at first, but curious, in that everything-you-do-is-interesting mood of a first date, which involved an Italian restaurant. By then she had also renounced white sugar, white flour and preservatives, which made an Italian restaurant difficult because of the pasta, but she could have the eggplant parmesan. Eventually Kurt had been easy to convert, especially after he discovered Tai Chi.

"By the way, I like sushi now. Actually just the taki—rice rolls with vegetables, I don't eat fish. Like what your mother made, that time when I wouldn't eat it . . .?"

"Did you meet my mother? I lived with my father and step-mother."

"She was Japanese."

"So is my mother."

"But who made the taki—rice rolls—that time?"

"I don't know, what time?"

Colin didn't have a hand cart or shopping basket, just several packages of something in one hand. He started to move down the aisle, but slowly, not walking away from her. "Are you going to pay . . . ?" Marcy asked from behind, before she caught up. A clunk from the lumber cart before she could finish with the word now.

"Yeah, this's all I need. We started the job but were missing just a few bolts, so I ran over."

Marcy was trying to get the lopsided cart to roll not-too-unevenly as she walked beside Colin. He was going slowly, as though to accommodate her efforts, but he went into a ten-items-or-fewer line, so Marcy checked out at the next register, a little surprised to find him waiting for her when she was finished, an orange Home Depot bag balled up in his hand. He didn't grab hold of Marcy's lumber cart, but again walked slowly beside it as she maneuvered out the sliding glass doors to the parking lot. Just outside the door, an employee checked their receipts.

Marcy started to laugh, but when Colin's small eyes still just gazed like shiny opaque stones out of his overly large face, she said, "Am I going to be able to guess your car from the bumper stickers?"

It turned out his car was a station wagon with a Baby On Board sign suction-cupped to the rear window. The car next to his—one of those tiny old Hondas that several boys could pick up and move from the parking lot to the sidewalk in high school—had a Nuke the Whales sticker. After graduating from high school during the second oil crisis, when people lined up for blocks to buy gas, Marcy tried to go without a car. She'd already answered a roommate needed ad in a weekly newspaper and moved in with a girl who turned out to be a born-again Christian. But the school Marcy went to that summer, to learn to be a bank teller, was across town from her new apartment and class started at 8 AM, so she'd bought a used Datsun that promised forty miles per gallon and made payments on it for a year. It was still their car—Kurt dropped her at work on his way—and her only bumper sticker was a fading Carter/Mondale. She and Kurt had been dating during the 1980 election, and Marcy had participated in door-to-door blitzes for the Carter campaign. She told Kurt if Reagan won, she was moving to a different country. On election day, she and Kurt were messing around on her bed with the radio playing an FM jazz station. She'd gotten off work at four and it was around five, not really dark yet, just almost. Suddenly the radio was announcing Carter's concession. "No!" Marcy had yelped, vaulting off the bed, "wait for me!" Fortunately, they weren't undressed yet. She and Kurt had run across the street to the VFW hall where the local polls were still open. When she remembers it, she thinks maybe they were both zipping their pants as they dashed into the voting booths. The next day at work, she'd dropped her purse into her drawer, slammed it with her shoe and announced, "Well, I'm moving to Canada." The other tellers looked up, most of them just airheads, bank robots— ATMs hadn't threatened anyone's job yet. That night, when Marcy's roommate was playing her Christian quasi-rock in the living room, Marcy and Kurt huddled in her room and decided to get married and rent a house so they wouldn't have to share walls with anyone who might have that or any other unsavory taste in music.

"Well . . . ," Colin said.

"Yeah, nice running into you."

"Yeah, I gotta go."

Marcy was shoving her lumber cart up the parking lane, not very far away yet, and Colin called, "Hey . . ." Marcy turned, bracing her weight to keep the cart from rolling back toward Colin. "I know why you were confused," he said. From that distance, his eyes were still just black spots, his face large and clammy looking, like he'd actually broken a sweat but hadn't noticed it yet. "My father got back together with my real mother. But wait, I think that was after high school. I can't remember. The only thing I cared about back then was not turning out like him."

After only a slight pause, Marcy said, "You did a good job."

Kurt had made his own peanut butter sandwich and went to his Tai-Chi lesson in the park. His note said, "I can make it there in time on the bus if I leave now." She thought he might call for her to pick him up, but they didn't have a cordless phone, and Marcy spent the afternoon making her fence, and luckily the spitty dog must have been locked inside. The hardest part was getting it to stand upright against the cinderblock wall by itself while she pounded the metal fence posts into the dirt. Also, the ground wasn't all that even, and in some places the bottoms of fence boards ground into the dirt; at others they hovered above, not touching. Something about where the weight was distributed and which part was absorbing the most pressure was off, but it was standing there, blocking the neighbor from looking or spraying his hose or throwing anything into her yard, and the fence was blocking his dog from barking at Marcy.

Kurt had called and left a message saying he was going out after class with the instructor and few others. He didn't say so, but Marcy knew they went out for tea, not beer, and talked about chess and another game called Go.

If Kurt had been there when she'd gotten home, she would've said, breathlessly laughing, "Guess what I found out about my high school boyfriend!" If he'd come home while she was still hammering nails or setting the fence upright, she would've snickered, "I saw my ex-boyfriend at Home Depot and guess what, he's fat." If he came home now, as she sat in the living room sipping orange juice, she might have said, "I saw an old boyfriend in Home Depot today." She finished the juice and went to take a nap.

The sound that woke her was, at first, like a thunderstorm. A loud crack. A thump on the roof. Two more thumps. Another crack. Some of the other commotion was unspecific, and she could hear the old alky neighbor's voice, but couldn't make out any words, as though he'd taken out his dentures and was having a fight with flapping gums. But an argument with who? His fleshy blousy wife who wore shapeless Hawaiian-print dresses, but who actually bothered to have a job? There was no second voice, but perhaps the other half of the argument was inside their house, and it was boomeranging back-and-forth to the outside, and the fallout was raining on the rest of the neighborhood. The front screen door bashed then shimmied for a second. More muffled thumps on the roof. Shattering of glass on concrete. Two, three, four more snap, crackle, pops. Bumps on the roof, and a vibrating, booming crash, like a gong, on the metal covering over Marcy's patio. Once during a halftime show, the band had played the 1812 Overture, and a special percussion section had been wheeled onto the field—huge bass drum for the cannon blasts, a gong for the explosions, chimes for the church bells, while off the field someone had tried to time fireworks to detonate at the right place in the music. Now as she tried to hum the melody of the 1812 Overture, to fit with the racket outside, Marcy remembered she had slipped a black glove over one white one, then raised her fist and left the football field in protest over the glorifying of war for entertainment, although the Earth Club had voted not to stage a demonstration that night since they needed to get student government money for their rain forest float in the homecoming parade. (After Marcy walked off the field, the faculty leader of the drill team had told her she was being replaced and suspended for a week, but Marcy decided that when she walked off she had also, right then, quit her position as captain.)

Everything became quiet, and Marcy counted inside her head. She got to a hundred, then two hundred, and it was still quiet. But she closed her eyes, waiting for more. The war in Vietnam had been over by the time Marcy got to high school, and not a single boy she knew would be drafted or go overseas to a battlefield, but she was thinking about Vietnamese villagers caught in the crossfire between Vietcong and American forces, hiding in their huts, counting the seconds between burst of shelling. But then again, the village was never just caught in an unfortunately located battle; the village was the battle, the village was the target.

Marcy padded in her socks through the living room into the kitchen. Through the kitchen door window, she saw a brown beer bottle in three pieces on her concrete patio. Two more brown bottles, whole, on the dirt in the yard that should be growing grass. Then, off to the side closer to the alky neighbor, she saw a broken piece of wood . . . then another, then another. Her whole fence was smashed, many of the upright cedar fence boards splintered off and tossed into her yard. The rest, a jagged snarl of fractured boards twisted askew but still attached to the two-by-four, lying flat, with more broken bottles glinting among the kindling.

Marcy backed up, squatted on the kitchen floor, breathing hard but not crying. If she could've called Kurt, she would've. But this was before cell phones, before pagers. Long before email and chat rooms and instant messaging. Before Columbine and Oklahoma City and OJ. She crawled back to the bedroom, shut the door and turned off the light, started a fan to create white noise, to drown out anything else she might've heard. And without sleeping, managed to not even hear Kurt come home until he flung open the bedroom door, demanding, "What the hell's going on? There's dog shit by the front door. Someone threw dog shit at the house."

"Dog shit too?" Marcy whispered.

"Yeah, it's all over the driveway."

"It's more than that," Marcy said softly, without moving, without turning toward Kurt. "The neighbor, he broke the fence I made, he threw bottles and trash into the yard. He went on some sort of rampage."

"You had to go and stick up a fence?"

"I told you why."

"Yeah, and now's when we should be calling the police, but we can't—he did this because you called the police."

"I was only trying to give us some privacy in our own yard."

"I don't go in the yard. I don't care about the yard. How about what happens here, in here? How come you're not obsessed with fixing what happens, or doesn't happen, in here?"

Marcy rolled to her back and looked at Kurt. He was very thin, had always been thin. He had narrow shoulders and a lean face. Once at a bank party, when someone said he was lucky he could eat whatever he wanted and not gain weight, someone else teasingly asked him if he'd been a POW. The two people had both been women.

"Please, Kurt, could you go pick it all up? I can't bear to look at it. Please . . . ?"

Kurt left, and over the fan Marcy didn't hear anything. Until, after a while, she heard the refrigerator open and close. She heard the mumble of the television on the other side of the wall. On Saturday at five, there were Kung Fu reruns. Grasshopper still wandered around the old West, spreading quiet wisdom, having women fall in love with his unflappable self, never succumbing to temptation, although she had wondered aloud to Kurt once, snickering, whether he boffed every one of them, but it just wasn't part of the storyline.

When Marcy came out to make something for supper, she peeked into the yard and didn't see any debris.

"What did you do with the dog shit?"

"Trash."

"What do you want for dinner?"

"Some of that dog shit sounds good."

"Want to just get burritos from the place on the corner?"

"I thought they had lard."

"Can't be any worse than dog shit."

The following week, on Saturday afternoon while Kurt was at Tai Chi, Marcy was taking a bag of indoor trash to the cans on the driveway, and the old alky neighbor was in his front yard again, with a hose. Her trash cans were around the side of the house nearest his. The bags of beer bottles and dog shit had departed with the trash pickup that week. Curbside recycling wouldn't begin for another year or two, so the beer bottles had gone into the regular trash. Ordinarily, Marcy would have insisted they keep the bottles and pieces of bottles separate and drive them over to the recycling center near the landfill, but she didn't say a word when the glass had clinked like chimes inside the bags as she carried them to the curb. The stack of splintered fence boards had been too much for one pick up and was still on the side of the house beside the cans, waiting to go into the trash little by little.

Marcy put her head down and started to skitter around the side of the house, but the neighbor called out, "Hey . . . hey, c'mere." Without his dentures again, his words as spitty as the dog's bark over the backyard cinderblock wall. Marcy looked up. The man gestured for her to come closer. He was wearing one of those pleated-down-the-front shirts, like a dentist smock. His salt-and-pepper hair was thick and longish, but lank and stringy. Marcy was coming nearer as slowly as she could. He gestured again, then dropped his hose. "C'mere, I want to show you something." Every 's' blew out some spit. Kurt had warned her not to antagonize him again. "Come around the fence," he said, so she did, coming around on the sidewalk to his front yard, and when she got there he was holding a shovel.

"I got something I want to give you," he said. "I'm so ashamed for what I did. I got something to give you."

"You don't have to give me anything."

"What I did was terrible, I want to give you something."

As he spoke, he was going around the side of his house, on the other side of the same cinderblock wall where Marcy had put her fence, but here it only came to her waist. She stopped to see how her yard looked from up here. It was a fairly complete view of everything: everything she'd planned to fix but hadn't yet, the dirt where grass should be, the bare embankment that could come sliding down, and the top side of the metal roof over the patio where she saw a faded green Frisbee and a deflated rubber ball that looked like a stomach. There were also four more brown bottles, several fist-sized rocks, and some grayish looking things that were obviously turds.

"Look there," the man said. Marcy turned away from the startling view of her own yard. The man was pointing with his shovel to the dirt beside the foundation of his house. A skinny rubbery plant was growing all alone there, with a few thick leaves and a long neck supporting one dark bruise-colored flower. "It's a black lily," he said. "They're very rare. You dig it up and take it to your yard."

"You don't have to give me this."

"Take it, because I did such a bad thing. I know I did a bad thing."

Marcy stared at the lily because she didn't want to look at the man's toothless mouth or the sweat starting to ooze from his hairline. She groped for the shovel and he put it into her hand. The dirt was hard, but she managed to get most of the shovel under the lily, in a circle all the way around, until the lily with its roots in a dirt clod were on the shovel, and she carried it home that way, then passed the shovel up to the man over the cinderblock wall. She dug a hole right there, beside the cinderblocks, and planted the black lily. Its neck was flaccid and the flower sagged to the ground.

Marcy never built the raised garden surrounded by picnic benches. She did put flagstones down where the lawn was mud, and she put a flower trellis up against the cinderblock wall, with a fast-growing jasmine to block the neighbor and his barking dog. But the neighbor shot his dog one night, the sound of the gun making Marcy bolt upright in bed while Kurt never stirred. Later that year, she would sit naked in a hot tub—at a former downtown motel remodeled to rent out dayrooms with saunas and Jacuzzis—beside a supervisor from the bank. She kept washing her mouth out with the chlorinated water between the times she went down on him, because there wasn't a lot of information on whether oral sex was safe. She wanted to be promoted from teller. The following spring, she was living in an apartment, alone, and the house had a For Sale sign by the time the black lily would have been sprouting again. On her last trip moving the last of her stuff, which Kurt had packed and left on the porch for her, she went into the house to leave a note for him. She didn't know what the note would say. She eventually left without writing it, but before that, she went through the kitchen and out to the yard to check the dirt beside the cinderblock wall for any sign of the black lily.

THE SIXTEEN PARTS

Maggie Greene

1

I knew it was good when, as David Gedge hit that high note, all I could imagine was sliding down on his cock. The first time it happened, I was walking down the stairs to the subway; on another I was riding home on the train and the blue seats leered at me, dirty thoughts in teal. Even when I still wasn't sure, the train told me it was good.

But to be clear: it isn't right. Good—not right. We talked about it the first weekend we went away together, in the hotel room in Portland. I asked him how he justified this to himself, how he explained it. He said, "I don't justify it, it isn't right. But when it's time for me to die, I want to—you know, if life is like a book, I want mine to be a good one. Usually I want to do what is right, but if I didn't do this I would regret it. No one wants to read a book where only good happens."

All the thoughts that go into an affair: the truth that it's unjustifiable, the fear of opportunities lost, the understanding that sometimes the best thing isn't right.

2

L., my boyfriend, knows. He knows the details: I love J. very much; J.'s cock is bigger; J. and I have so much more in common. He knows when I am with J. and he knows what we talk about, even when we talk about him. Our relationship is only better for it—good spaces make good partners.

J.'s wife doesn't know. When we first got together, I would begin falling asleep next to L., feeling richer than Ruskin, then wake myself wondering how J. could feel, laying there in the standardized domestic dream, with his wife and children and recliner, loving me. My love for J., open, cleaved L. and I. His for me could cleave him and a wife he adores. It really pisses me off.

3

On reconnaissance, J.'s marriage is the Maginot Line, an ineffective yet theoretically spectacular defense. For my part, I am my own fascist horde, inclined against marriage to begin with. My mother isn't married, and like most unholy bastard spawn, I never understood the big deal; having a second parent seemed like having a twin— interesting but inessential. We were two and that was enough.

Then came Simone de Beauvoir. I found out about her in high school, and from the start it made sense, her relationship with Sartre and its inherent reaffirmation of freedom. To be really independent, she had to be free to desire for herself, not just free to work and think; yet there was the security of one who knew all her history, the one who didn't need background. I saw it all then and I wanted that. I know now that it wasn't so easy for them, but when I was fifteen, it seemed to be.

4

When I met L., his open marriage—yes, there is something about me that attracts married men, and no, I don't know what it is—was falling apart, was essentially over. I have never been entirely sure what was happening—those two were moving apart, they wanted different things, they didn't know how to talk about it. It had nothing to do with me. We never an affair and I wasn't a secret. And because of the openness that let me in, L. and I were unrestricted from the beginning, though only theoretically at first. L. was the first man to really fall in love with me and I was too scared to lose him. A pudgy, bitchy late-bloomer, I was astounded anyone could love me and figured I better hang on. (Sometimes I still wonder if I first fell in love with him just because he could love me, my own thoughts remaining unnecessary.)

L. refrained from seriously pursuing anyone else for the first few years, though we did occasionally sleep with other people— usually when one or the other of us was out of town. In fact, for a good part of the first few years we sequestered ourselves. There is a place for monogamy, especially in building a good foundation. But when J. came along, I didn't have to keep the monogamy and watch it molder. Unlike him, I didn't have to hold on to monogamy and let it threaten to rot my whole primary relationship.

J. would never put it that way. He loves his wife and his marriage, and he doesn't cheat because he wants out. He cheats because he wants in to another love—the underlauded second sort. He said he could juggle and from the start he has. But it kills me that he has to. He isn't a bad guy, and I'm not bad either. We don't want to walk away from our others and we can't walk away from one another.

On my end, that's okay. L. knows he can't be everything to me, and doesn't want to be. One of our oldest conflicts has centered on how much intense attention each of us needs. Now, L. can go out and do all the things I don't want to do with people I don't want to talk to. I can stay in my bed, suffused with affection, and watch my own desire rise like steam.

In between these two men, I am happy. J., though, takes such a risk to make me feel this way. Together we might hurt someone who doesn't deserve to be hurt, but who has managed to get herself into this position by demanding all or nothing, then taking an oath to that in public. For love we imperil someone who can't even benefit from that love the way L. has. Pretending desire can be shut off, criminalizing it—it makes something lovely and amoral, dangerous.

5

J. is not being disloyal; loyalty assumes sides, and there are no sides here. I am not competing with his wife. Besides keeping a running list of reasons I'm glad not to be married to him (a joke only I find funny), I have encouraged J. to be a better husband. While sweaty and panting in my bed, I have reminded him to go home and fuck his own wife in their bed, even if she is a worn-out mommy with no time—because she is a worn-out mommy with no time and needs to feel hot, too. I want her to know about this; I want her to see how her husband's love for someone else redoubles love back at her. If only she could know that the idea of him fucking her is so hot to me. I cherish him in that position. It's like giving someone a bite of your tasty dinner: so good you have to share.

But no. She bought into some contract she was—we all are—told to want. And now what could be an occasion for generosity is an occasion for outcomes better not considered. Because if she finds out, it will be a competition. He will only be able to have one, and I can't say I want to win. Then again, I wouldn't want to lose.

I don't blame her personally for this; I don't blame her for wanting him forever.

6

Marriage deserves to be unraveled for all the reasons that anyone in an affair would say: It creates shortages of the things most people never stop hoping for. Marriage degrades us by sealing grace and almost wishes its own collapse with unreasonable expectations and shoddy construction. It is a testament to human ingenuity that something as crappy as marriage can endure; imagine if that genius for getting by could be funneled into a better structure.

Desire, which becomes the flaw in marriage, is at the center of any affair. The prosaic details knit the primary relationship. The absence of these bills and baths stick the affair; being removed gives it its existential difference.

7

The beginning of our first weekend together as I can tell it in public: [Name deleted] and I drove [direction changed] to [unnamed city]. We stayed at the [name altered] Hotel, in [neighborhood we would never find appealing, to confuse you]. It was near [someplace totally different], and we walked there for dinner. When we got back to the hotel, we stayed up till late, curled around each other and comfortable. At that late hour, we had that conversation everyone does, where you find that you are totally alike and destined to be together. We discovered we both worried about being assholes, feared we wouldn't amount to as much as we could for pissing people off.

[Name deleted] and I both wish we could manage to be likable and commiserated over our lack of inclination to agreeability.

All the identifiers are gone, these places and names are parts of us, but what's left is all that shit we treasure: Endless variations on personal connection that are the stuff of both commercials and arias. Thus the attraction of the long-term affair is that it creates a space without the weight of the exterior. With the details of life banished except as recollection, hopes and woes are foregrounded in a way real life never allows.

When things are off—without the ceremonial male head in residence—when they are unofficial, unsanctioned, you know people are there because they really want to be. When you undo a big rule, pettier constraints disappear as well; everything is both lighter and richer.

Like parallel households with their similar bones and divergent flesh, the affair mimics and perverts the structure of marriage. Both attain power in denial, but while marriage is by definition the willed renunciation of further desire, the affair gains power because it disturbs nothing without, though within the lovers succumb. The first is a public act sanctified by a specific denial; it is love exposed to all. The second is illuminated by its surrender, its ultimate indulgence, but only for two. When this all began and I first faced the possible ramifications and misery for all involved, only abandon stared back. I don't care what happens tomorrow if I may kiss him tonight, I thought. If I can hear him whisper, "yes I said yes I will Yes," upon a leather banquette, the chilly morning will be endured. If something could burn so hot, the embers were bound to remain.

8

Affairs are kind of fucked too.

First obstacle is time. Again, contrary to marriage where the time is specified by vows—till death do us part—is nearly infinite, there is never enough time in an affair. You are, after all, hiding from someone you live with. The bonus in this is that the I-must-see-you-as-soon-and-as-often-as-I-can stage lasts much longer with your amant; here is another case of boundaries making experience more intense. Yet, however much nostalgia the idea of this stage brings on, living through a burning desire to see someone isn't really so fun. The two hours here, three hours there, glory-be-we-can-manage-six schedule becomes frustrating. By the time it does, your affair has moved beyond the new fuck into deep affection: You can't turn away.

So I muddle through, sometimes sad, often unsatisfied, but unabashedly in; for J. and I, scheduling is easier than for most. We both have flexible work situations, leaving afternoon trysts the staple. He comes over to my apartment, we fuck and talk, and then it's time to shower and go. This is extraordinarily pleasant. It is also extremely limited. Within a rigid off-hour schedule, there is no time for adventure or serendipity. When I watch *Butterfield 8* (a great affair movie with a terrible ending—why does the homewrecker always have to die?), I can't imagine how Liz Taylor and her love can just walk the streets of Manhattan, shopping. In this world, that is both dangerous (people who know your wife shop, too) and unlikely. Going to the zoo would require the precision of an airstrike. As for serendipity, serendipity is how you get caught. No light surprises, no sweet accidents. This is a deliberate act all through.

Together, time constraints and schedules can turn the hothouse into an unventilated chamber. The same features that set an affair apart can keep life from getting in. If something important happens to J., neither the mourning nor the celebration can get in. Instead the faintest traces curl above, emotions abstracted and nearly motionless.

9

There begins the comparison: the chilliest part of all. When two people occupy similar roles, it is only natural to compare them, instinctively if not explicitly. This function is at the center of most affair-phobia, and it is difficult to stop.

Furthermore, the newer one too often comes out on top. Dissatisfaction festers. The sex suffers. In my case, it was slightly worse. L. is my first and only long-term relationship. Before him, I wondered with an unfortunate regularity whether I was lovable at all; after J., I worried I had settled. If someone could find me so appealing that he would go to great risk to have me, what was I doing in this threadbare spring-in-the-ass relationship?

At the point when this question threatened to become unbearable, I shared my thoughts with L. and the oddest thing happened: as soon as ambivalence became word, the ambivalence disappeared. The affair folded back for a moment, and in the face of renouncing L., I found my love staring back.

It is possible that things won't work out this way for everyone. One might not find love there. But that won't be the lover's fault. As Simon Blackburn observes in an essay on lust, "Someone might want to have sex for many reasons: to have children, to prove that they can do it, to gratify a partner, simply to be rid of someone, to advance their career, to provide a medical sample, or to earn some money." Just as easily, one can have an affair for a number of reasons, only one of which is to tweeze out an excuse to leave. Though convenient, an affair is a spectacularly awful way to leave another: The negative space left by the one before is certain to dent the tension and dement the affair; to leave a partnership for an affair is to abscond with a mirage. In this way, the nature of an affair does manage to defuse one of its dangers, as long as one can enter into it with a sense of self-knowledge and a smidgen of wisdom. A lack of awareness can doom one to wander unsatisfied amidst comparison, but a lack of awareness leads to mistakes in any number of endeavors, and we don't condemn all saws just because one person cuts off his hand.

As our affair proceeds, it becomes clearer and clearer that J. and I would be miserable as one another's only only. J. wants a wife; so much of what he is able to manage to do every day is facilitated by someone else taking care of the home and food and children. I have no interest in being a wife, for either J. or L. In fact, it is L. who helps me, bringing dinner when I am working, picking up things I don't have time to fetch. Both J. and I are the selfish ones in our relationships; already there are moments when his work calls break into our time (that precious, hard-to-come-by, actual time). I can manage in this case—all this is just a beyond—but I wouldn't put up with it as my life. To be entirely together in that prosaic world would require one of us to back down, yet it is our selfishnesses that come together so well in this abstract world.

10

It is easy to see this affair as a different kind of sharing, I think, because J. and I both began by making it entirely clear that neither of us was looking for a teammate replacement. And, oddly enough for something built out of dishonesty, this relationship only manages itself for being radically honest, more honest than a number of primary relationships I'm privy to. L. and I have had this reinforce us because we are honest about it. I regret J.'s necessary deception, for the stress it causes us, for the harm it threatens his wife—but full openness? Ick.

Full openness immediately makes me imagine those polyamorous communities with sex schedules on the fridge and endless processing. Exposing J.'s and my twisted manner of affection to full light would be certain to shrivel it. Just the thought makes me itch to scurry under said icebox. Hiding out at a mediocre hotel in Baltimore is only fun when it is slightly naughty. There is freedom in the unattached "I" that shouldn't be undone. I want J. to be able to tell his wife about us, but I don't want to lose the fulfilling melancholy of our rainy afternoons, so dear for knowing we should be elsewhere, doing other—useful—things.

The bubble of an affair can keep desire dangerous. I can call in sick and snuggle some Wednesday with L., but that seems like a

women's magazine recommendation. It is something I ought to do:
Take a little time out with my lover. But where, then, is the halfway
tension that would make the desire for a second love possible—per-
missible—without desiccating it?

11

One possibility would be to build one-by-one relationships in
which we could admit our desire to our closed circle of lovers, but
to continue to lie to our parents, our bosses, and everyone else. It
would be naughty without threatening those closest. It would also
be incredibly stupid. We spend our entire lives attempting to
explain our idiosyncrasies and assimilate those of others; why pretend this incredibly human thing is unlikely? Besides, to act as if
affairs are unhealthy and to be discouraged is to cede the argument
on desire before beginning. Blackburn says, "If we associate lust
with excess and surfeit, then its case is already lost." Similarly, if
we associate extramarital relationships with excess and surfeit, we
concede that human desire ought only to content itself with a single other (after a series of tryouts). What a narrow, ugly, blinkered
view of human sexuality.

Besides, I am not a liar. The fact that I tell lies to get this relationship disgusts me. But I will not turn away. This is not surplus
to me. Being with J. has done more to make me feel like a true
human, has done more to illuminate the stranger—and by that I
mean the most mundane—aspects of our common condition than
any arbitrary code. I do not find it odd that in this situation I
would want to modify the code, rather than us.

12

In truth, what I really want of the code is understanding, some
complexity. It feels strange to ask for complexity from my ethics;
normally I am of simpler moral bent: I think killing people is wrong
no matter what, so I don't kill people. I don't think this changes
across situations; even if I am threatened, I will not do violence. But
perhaps this is not so big as killing. Perhaps, in fact, it is not the
action that does violence in this case, but the code that names the
action violent that makes it wound. Wait, did I say perhaps? I was
trying to understate. It didn't work.

13

The code lies. The contract lies. The society that tells us this is the only contract fibs us into misery. So how about we replace the lies with some acknowledgements: People will not be content to desire only one person over decades. A mistress is not a wife. A good mistress does not want to replace a wife and is not competition for a wife. Both mistress and wife are reasonable choices. An affair needs secrecy, and so should not be as exposed as a marriage; being subterranean, however, does not make one wrong.

14

Because relationships are made in time, constant philandering is less desirable than a long-term extramarital relationship. Building itself around a heightened desire, a good affair is the antithesis of the ultimately futile cycle of amorous hunger quickly sated. A marriage is an adventure in companionship; as years and troubles pass, lust dampens and camaraderie deepens into the pleasures of well-aged affection. A good, long affair is an adventure in desire; as it progresses, lust unfurls into its rarer shapes. It is not a simple meal eaten over and again in exact detail, dulling the one appetite and tarnishing others. This is worthwhile in a way that gobbling sex is not.

15

From these acknowledgements, we can perhaps move into the creation of a social atmosphere wherein desire is treated more appropriately. We can build a conversation around more interesting aspects of this whole business, such as: What else makes a good extramarital relationship? What is the best way to balance the needs of mistress and wife (or cuckold and cuckolder)? When people are married, what will they stipulate in their particular contract? What kind of marriage suits different temperaments the best? Paths will multiply, and instead of impoverishing ourselves for lack of choices, we can perhaps begin to acknowledge that choices are there to be made.

16

Affirming that there are options, by the way, does not make every choice equal. In choosing my affair now, I have chosen to be the sort of person who sees variations on desire, who sees individual desires that deserve to write themselves.

Reading *The Second Sex* made me proud of my mind, which conferred an ownership of self I never could have felt otherwise. Now I'd like to form the kind of culture where I can have the same sort of pride in—and ownership of—my desire. I want that for me, for L., for J. I want it above all for his wife, a woman who doesn't deserve the threats manufactured by lies.

MINIATURE BRIDGES, YOUR MOUTH

Marty McConnell

what we do in the dark has no hands. no
crossover effect, no good-bye kiss after the alarm.
what we carry in, we carry out, end of story. this
doesn't even want to be love. except in minutes
when your face has the shape of my palm and I think
lungful. let want out with the cat. returns
and returns, something dutiful. persistent.
hold your breath, let it build, let go. this is practice.
I'm losing weight, a bad sign, I'm happy. serious,
you say. contained, I think. the cat comes back
with a dead bird to the doorstep, an offering. bloodless
this should be easy. a two-step to cowboys. you're beautiful
but that's not the point.

x

I know my way back perfectly well. like the back
of my hand, as it were. but look, the labyrinth walls
are high hedge and green. this also could be joy.

xx

I literally don't know your middle name. does that
matter? what systems we arrange for intimacy, small
disclosures like miniature bridges, your mouth. not
what I'd anticipated. softer. to begin with,
I should tell the truth more. I could miss you,
and that's a liability.

xxx

I'm not often off-kilter. but you're so silent, even
naked, and almost absent. I hush too, why
are we here. go. want to throw things, you, the clock,
break windows until something bleeds and you finally
scream. I tell you too much; we are not
those people. or nothing—maybe I say
utilitarian fuck. how would that be. I want you
to want to fall in love with me and that's
unhealthy. wrong. leave your shoes by the door
and pretend it's about the movie. it's love
in the movies it's casablanca and toy story
and water no ice come here. pockets need
to be untucked, drawers thrown open,
nobody's safe. there, I've said it:
somebody I was could have loved you.

BEATING AROUND
THE BURNING BUSH

Matthue Roth

I'm cheating on my girlfriend with G-d.

I came home late last night, Friday night, still in my dress clothes from work. My clothes smelled of candle wax, sweet-bread challah was on my breath. I felt the compulsion to buy a box of Tic-Tacs and swallow them all. The classic compulsion of cheating: as much as you try to cover up, you can never cover up enough.

But I passed the WaWa, feeling the change roll around in my pockets, knowing I can't. Buying Tic-Tacs would be a business transaction, and we don't work, not on the L-rd's Day.

Even if it's to cover up?

Now it's early Saturday morning and I'm writing this in my head, knowing if I write it down I'll lose it all.

I'll lose her, I mean. And I'll lose Him too.

Everything.

When I got home that night, she didn't say anything. Gave me this look like *I know where you've been.* My first reaction was to check, not my neck for lipstick, but the soulspot at the back of my head for a yarmulke. I didn't feel anything but hair. But I still felt this look. *She knows where I've been.*

She doesn't, though, not really. I mean—she grew up Catholic.

She swishes off her business suit, lets down her hair. "I'm going to bed," she calls. "Will you shut the lights when you're done down here?"

When I woke up this morning, they were still on.

First day: I throw out all the pots while she's at work. I drive to Target and purchase an identical set so she won't notice. I drive to Safeway and go grocery shopping: Everything I buy has a kosher seal.

G-d and me, we send each other secret messages. We have to talk in code so my girlfriend doesn't get suspicious. There are love notes written all over the packages: A K inside a circle. A K inside a triangle. Hebrew letters that I don't understand, the microscopic squiggle next to the ® sign saying, it's kosher, G-d approves of it. Driving home, the trunk is full of ketchup bottles and mayonnaise jars nearly identical—but for the kosher marks—to the condiments we already own. I called them love notes but, I realize now, they could just as well be threatening letters from G-d: *Eat my food or suffer*.

My girlfriend comes home at sunset, donning her white apron to cook dinner, the one with the frills. Rummaging through the fridge, she picks up the new ketchup bottle—the one I strategically emptied to the level of our old ketchup bottle—and examined it in the light. "Honey," she calls, "do we normally buy Heinz?"

"It was a sale," I reply quickly.

Too quickly.

These are the things I want to tell her: The way it feels to pray. When G-d screams my name. The times that we are huddled together, after my girlfriend leaves for work and G-d comes in, presses His hand on my breast, rustles the hair on my head and the hairs on my chest and the words that come out of my mouth are not my own. They are half script and half speaking in tongues. That's what I want to tell her: Sometimes I feel like I'm possessed.

And I think I like being possessed.

Third day: She finds out.

"Why are you doing this, honey?" she asks.

She isn't mad. I want her to be mad. I want her to grab me by the lapel, throw me on the wall and shake me, screaming that I have to make a choice, her or G-d. In my fantasy, she stands on one side, G-d stands on the other side. You can't see G-d because He's G-d.

My girlfriend says, "Make a choice."

G-d says, "Obey me."

I tell her, "I have to take a walk." As soon as I'm outside I start praying.

I think I was born to be controlled.

Fourth day: She's on the Internet, spying on the competition. She checks out the bookmarks I've made, kept in a password-protected folder. The password wasn't that hard to guess. G-d has many names, but most of them are in other languages.

She looks at me, that same look, a measure of vacancy and pity.

I close my eyes, expecting the floodgates to burst open like Niagara Falls.

Instead, only her eyes fall.

She is standing in the kitchen, refrigerator door open, the light crinkling on and off. In the soft palm of her hand she is fondling the block of orange American cheese I bought from the kosher supermarket.

She says: "Sweetie, why didn't you tell me? We can work this out."

No, we can't. You don't know G-d like I do. There's nothing to work out. This will only end in earthquakes and ranting and prophecies of doom.

She hugs me.

She says, "It's all I can do."

Day four ends as we settle into our bed and I snake my limbs around her body, feeling in every inch of her warm skin betrayal, castigation, and eventual repentance. Day four, at close: Uneasily at peace.

Fifth day: Today we walk on eggshells. We eye each other like we've got secrets, and I guess we do. Over breakfast, the only noise is spoons stirring cereal. Over dinner, the same thing. We sit in the living room at night, pretending to read books, so quiet we could be praying.

Sixth day: The sun creeps between the Venetian blinds of our shared apartment like a warning. She unwraps herself from me, dons clothes, goes to work. As soon as she's gone I roll out of bed, pour water on my hands in the ritually prescribed manner—three times over the left hand, three times over the right—and wrap the leather straps around my body. I'm learning to obey. I'm learning to get better. There are two hundred and forty-eight positive commandments, but three hundred and sixty-five negative ones, and I'm trying to follow every one, but I'm trying to make her the last one to go.

Every time I touch her I'm cheating on G-d.

Most religions demand you devote your soul. I'm an Orthodox Jew. In our system of belief, it doesn't matter if you believe. What matters is devoting your body.

Everything.

The foods we are permitted to ingest. When we excrete, we say prayers. The hour we wake in the morning. The songs we sing when we can't fall asleep at night (chapters of psalms, starting with the number that corresponds to your age, continuing from there). I lay beside her last night, unable to sleep, afraid to touch her because I was reciting psalms in my head and I thought if our skin came into contact G-d might hear. I'm dreading the onslaught of tonight: At sunset, the sixth day becomes the seventh. Sabbath. The day G-d rested, and so do we.

When we enter the bedroom her face is painted muted brush strokes, a resigned look in her eyes. She peels off her clothes and ducks under the covers, snuggling the blankets, blinking at me expectantly.

I stand there in the doorway, frozen, knowing the last commandment I've been able to ignore: not to touch any woman except my wife.

"What's wrong?"

She blinks at me.

"I—I'm sorry." I don't even know how to stutter right anymore.

I turn, ashamed, and run from the room. That night I sleep on the couch, blanketless, alone.

Seventh day: It's her day off work. This used to be the day we spent together.

Instead, it's the day I slip away.

Inside the synagogue nobody recognizes me and that's fine. I wear a black suit so I won't blend in. The words that leap to my lips, unbidden and Tourettes-like, sound exactly like the words everyone else is singing. I don't think about how I know the words, how they sound, or how to pronounce these letters that look more like karmic sex positions. In the sanctuary, everyone sits, facing the ark, and then at one point the cantor's voice rises to a shrill, his hands cupped skyward like a solar generator, mouth forming the vertically ovular O like he's being sucked off under his robes. At that point, every man in the congregation sings the words as a melody in unison, shooting out of their seats, and I jump up too, shaking my body back and forth above my waist like I'm fucking something invisible in the air before me, shaking with religious frenzy, singing higher and louder than anyone else around, loud enough so people start to notice my mispronunciation of the linguistic nuances, dropping their prayerbooks to stare, but I don't stop. I couldn't, even if I wanted to. I'm praying, singing out my love letters heavenward, and I hope to G-d that everybody in that room is watching.

BELONGING IMPOSSIBLE, LONGING ALL THERE IS

Susannah Breslin

The relationship between the husband and the wife was in a bad state. The husband had cheated on the wife. Now, there were a great many walls between them. Something had to be done. One day, the wife woke up, and when the husband went to work, she went to the store around the corner. There, she bought herself a sledgehammer. She took the sledgehammer home, wrapped in a sheet of brown paper, and with it knocked down all the interior walls of the apartment in which they lived. That night, the husband returned home. He was surprised to find the mess the wife had made of their life. There was dust everywhere—in her hair, in his gin and tonic, in his underwear drawer. Over dinner, the husband asked the wife what she had done. The wife shrugged her shoulders and smiled at the husband as if to ask what else could she have done? At this, the husband realized he was sorry. From that point onward, the husband decided he would be true to her. Afterwards things were better. The husband and the wife could see each other when they were at home in their apartment; it was hard to hide anything from one another when everything could be seen. Eventually, the wife returned the sledgehammer to the store, explaining to the young man working behind the counter why she didn't need it anymore, and the young man, for his part, was helpful and obliging, as if he understood what the wife was saying, even though the young man was soft in a way that reminded the wife of the husband years ago. Later, the wife found herself in the storage room of the store, her rear end situated atop an unvarnished wooden workbench, where she was, it appeared, having sex with the young man from behind the counter. Then, the wife went home. In a way, she felt better, as if, somehow, things had swung back into balance, but she also felt worse, as if what had swung back into balance had, at the same time, lost its moorings altogether. She considered this as she made dinner. The husband was sitting in his armchair at the other end of the apartment with no walls. He appeared to be reading, but he was watching her from over the top of the newspaper that he was pretending to read. There was something different about her, he knew, and while he suspected it was unfamiliar to her, it was familiar to him. The wife looked over her shoulder at the husband, across the great expanse of space between them, and she recognized that she did not know what this situation was or what to do about it. The wife turned away from the husband. She went into the bathroom, the last room with walls. The husband came to the door and told the wife to come out, but she did not; she did not even reply. Instead, the wife sat on the lowered toilet seat lid, her chin on her palm, thinking about how while it had seemed on the outside that things had gotten better, she had come to find that on the inside, things were not better at all. The husband stood on the other side of the door, listening to whatever it was that the wife was doing. The wife picked up a small dictionary sitting on the tank of the toilet, and she began reading out loud from it, making her way through the As. When she arrived at the word "adultery," she paused, and she could hear the husband breathing on the other side of the door. Here was the entry and the meaning of the word, and she read it loudly, as if she was trying to make some kind of a point. On the page, she could see, there was an illustration of an adulterer, a companion for the words that described it. She looked at the drawing, and she realized it was a portrait of herself, although, when she closed her eyes and opened them again, the drawing looked like her husband. It was hard to tell. On the other side of the door, the husband was frightened; the words the wife had spoken made him anxious, but the silence that had followed was unbearable. He asked the wife why she wouldn't come out so they could talk about this like adults. The wife heard what the husband was saying, but she didn't want to do that. There was nothing adult about any of this, especially when she had been in the storage room with her legs spread wide amidst all that white plumbing, feeling like she was fourteen again. The husband could hear the desperation in his voice as his words bounced off the bathroom door and back at him. It was impossible, he feared, to reach her. The wife stood in front of the bathroom mirror. She balanced the dictionary on her head like a beauty queen and pirouetted once, sticking out her tongue at the bathroom door. On the other side of the door, the husband fell to his knees, and, through the keyhole, demanded to know what she was doing. The wife got on her knees at the door, and she could see the eye of the husband peering in at her through the keyhole. With one hand snaking up the wall, she turned the bathroom light on and off, watching the husband's pupils contract and dilate as she did so. She had a powerful effect on him, located at such a deep level that even he could not control it. In the past, this knowledge had kept her company, but she felt sad and lonely with it in the bathroom. The wife went to the tub and turned on both faucets, creating a racket that drowned out the husband. As the tub filled, the wife focused all her energies on ignoring the small person inside herself who wanted to turn the doorknob and let her husband into this interior of hers. She had to do something; she knew this. So, the wife took off all her clothes, unlocked the door, ran across the bathroom floor, and leapt into the tub, submerging herself under the surface of the water. In one hand, she held a tampon insertion device, devoid of its tampon, above the water level. Through it, the wife breathed like the deep-sea snorkeler she knew she could become if she dumped all this and moved to Australia, or Fiji, or some place like that. There, the wife lay, staring at the ceiling. The husband's face entered the frame of her vision. The husband was talking to the wife, but she couldn't understand what he was saying because the only thing she could hear was the vast nothingness of water pressing in upon her, making her feel safe, which was all she had ever really wanted in life. If it was water that would be there for her in this, then water would be it. The wife watched the husband's mouth say the letter *I*, then *M*, then *S*, then *O*, then *R*, then another *R*, and then a *Y*. She was angry, self-sunk in this sea of hers, because *Y* was it, wasn't it? Why her husband had done this, why she had done this, why they had come to this, her with a tampon insertion device in her mouth and him apologizing to her over a toilet. She could stay like this for the rest of her life, coming out only to de-prune and loll about on the bathroom rug, but it was possible if she did so that one night, gazing out the bathroom window to stare at the moon and think about the boy at the store, she might see the boy below her in the halo of a streetlamp, walking home with a young girl tucked under his arm, and the only thing she would be able to do would be to toss a roll of toilet paper out the window at him. Here, at least, the husband was sorry. The wife moved the tube to her eye so she could see the husband better through this periscope of hers. It looked like he was crying, for there was something falling from his eyes, but the wife couldn't tell if it was tears or not, since she, herself, was in the water. She had to know. She sat up in the bathtub, and she threw the tampon insertion device across the room. The husband stood limp before her. The only thing he knew was that he didn't know what he knew anymore or what to do about it. The wife waited. Slowly, the husband peeled off his clothes, and he climbed into the tub, sitting in the water across from the wife, so the two of them faced one another. There they were, this husband and this wife, two piles of skin stretched over taut muscles hung on fragile bones. He had done something terrible, put himself out for sale on a fluorescent-lit supermarket aisle like a package of chicken parts, all pink flesh and yellow skin, and some woman had come along, eyed his price tag, checked his expiration date, and thrown him into her basket. He had gone home with her, laying himself upon her plate, sacrificing himself to this cannibal of their marriage, making a totemic feast of their life. Still, the husband and the wife knew there was something here between them, something more than dim bags of meat and bone. They had slipped out of one body, into the arms of others, and discovered, within these four walls, they only had each other. They were intertwined like legs under a table, on loan to each other between God and the grave, two books checked out from the library with a debt to be repaid. Belonging impossible, longing all there is, he was the man of her days, she was the apple of his eyes and it was in each other's company that they hoped they would one day die.

ABOUT THE CONTRIBUTORS

S. Bear Bergman is a theater artist, writer, instigator, and gender-jammer. Ze has touring hir award-winning shows *Ex Post Papa* and *Clearly Marked* around the country to colleges, universities and theater festivals, including the National Gay and Lesbian Theater Festival and the National Transgender Theater Festival. Ze has been heard and published in a variety of places, lives on the Web at www.sbearbergman.com, and makes a home in Northampton, Massachusetts, where ze is the very lucky husbear of a magnificent femme.

Susannah Breslin is the author of *You're a Bad Man Aren't You?* from Future Tense Books. She is currently at work on a semi-autobiographical novel, *If Only These Hands Could Talk*, based on her experiences in Porn Valley.

Eli Brown lives and writes in Oakland, California. He received a master's degree in creative writing from Mills College and has recently completed a novel about seduction and corruption in a cult compound. More of his poetry can be read online at www.cortlandreview.com.

Stephen Burt is taking names. He and Jessie and their cats used to live in Manhattan, all the way up the A at 207th Street; now they live in St. Paul, Minnesota, across from the state fairgrounds, because Macalester College hired him, for which he remains appropriately grateful. Stephen Burt endorses and depends on the music of Amelia Fletcher, the post play of Janel McCarville and/or Vanessa Hayden, and the feminist psychoanalytic arguments of Jessica Benjamin. His books of poetry include *Popular Music*

(CLP/Colorado, 1999) and *Parallel Play* (Graywolf, 2006); his web site is www.accommodatingly.com.

Stephen Elliott is the author of the novel *Happy Baby* and the political memoir *Looking Forward To It*.

Gina Frangello is the executive editor of *Other Voices* magazine and its new book imprint, OV Books. Her short fiction has appeared in many literary venues, most recently *Story Quarterly*, *Blithe House Quarterly*, *Prairie Schooner,* and *Hawaii Review*. She guest-edited the anthology *Falling Backwards: Stories of Fathers and Daughters* (Hourglass, 2004). She is a frequent freelancer for the *Chicago Reader*, and has contributed book reviews to the *Chicago Tribune*. In 2002, she was the recipient of an Illinois Arts Council fellowship for prose. She received her MA in the Program for Writers at the University of Illinois at Chicago, has taught literature and creative writing at various universities in Chicago, and recently completed a novel.

Barry Graham is a journalist, screenwriter, poet and the author of five books of fiction. His nonfiction has appeared in a variety of magazines, including *Harper's*. Born in Scotland, he has traveled widely and now lives in Tennessee, between a mental hospital, a sewage plant, and an American Indian burial ground.

Maggie Greene wishes she could tell you who she is.

Christine Hamm has a MA in creative writing and is a graduate of Reed College. Her poetry has been published by *Poetry Midwest*, *can we have our ball back?*, *Kitchen Sink, Snowmonkey, Rattle*, the *Absinthe Literary Review*, the *Adirondack Review* and many others. She was also a finalist in the Atlanta Review International Poetry Contest. In 2004, she was nominated for a Pushcart Prize. She teaches poetry workshops in New York City and is the literary editor of several journals.

Jonathan Harper has never worked in a bookstore! But he did graduate from George Mason University with a BA in English and creative writing in May 2002 and is now the assistant managing editor of the Lambda Literary Foundation. He has been published on www.defenestrationmag.net.

Michael Hemmingson is thirty-something, has published thirty-plus books, and lives in San Diego. He edited, for Soft Skull, *What the Fuck: the Avant-Porn Anthology*. He's also co-edited *Expelled from Eden: A William T. Vollmann Reader* and *The Mammoth Book of Short Erotic Novels*. Some of his own novels include *Wild Turkey, The Rose of Heaven, House of Dreams,* and *The Comfort of Women.*

David A. Hernandez's first collection, *A House Waiting for Music*, was published by Tupelo Press in 2003. His poems have appeared in *Southern Review, TriQuarterly, Iowa Review, Epoch, Indiana Review, Agni,* and *Mississippi Review.* David is married to writer Lisa Glatt. Visit his web site at www.davidahernandez.com.

Thomas Hopkins is a writer who, as of this writing, lives in Brooklyn.

Merri Lisa Johnson is the editor and contributing author of *Jane Sexes It Up: True Confessions of Feminist Desire* (Four Walls Eight Windows, 2001) and is currently co-editing a collection of essays by and about strippers called *Flesh for Fantasy: Producing and Consuming Exotic Dance* (Avalon, 2005). She is an assistant professor of English at Coastal Carolina University, where she teaches American literature, autobiography, and women's studies.

Cris Mazza's most recent books are *Disability, Homeland,* and a memoir titled *Indigenous/Growing Up Californian.* Among her other notable titles are *Dog People, Girl Beside Him,* and the critically acclaimed *Is It Sexual Harassment Yet?* She is a professor in the Program for Writers at the University of Illinois at Chicago.

Marty McConnell tries to release the poems that huddle between the world we travel and the one we battle to create. She received her MFA from Sarah Lawrence College and co-curates a weekly reading series through The louderARTS Project, a literary nonprofit organization where she serves as programming director. She spent 2004 travelling with the Declare Yourself! youth voter empowerment campaign and performs at colleges and festivals around the country, including the Dodge Poetry Festival, Connecticut Poetry Festival, and more. Her work has appeared in

14 Hills, 13th Moon, Blue Fifth Review, Lodestar Quarterly, and numerous anthologies.

Lenelle Moïse is an out, Haitian-American poet, playwright, and performance artist. She is winner of the 2003 New WORLD Theater Poetry Slam and a recipient of the James Baldwin Memorial Award in Playwriting. She also recieved an MFA from Smith College. Lenelle's plays include *The Many Faces of Nia, Spilling Venus, Lesbians Talking About RICE, Purple,* and *Cornered in the Dark.* She co-wrote *Sexual Dependency*, a feature-length film about cross-cultural machismo by Bolivian director Rodrigo Bellot. She is also a commissioned writer for *We Got Issues*, a performance-based dialogue about young women and voting. She recites radical poetry at universities, progressive bookstores and quirky theatres across the United States, and has twenty-four-year-old dreams in Northampton, Massachussetts. For more info, please visit www.lenellemoise.com.

Neal Pollack is the happily married author of three books, a satire column for *Vanity Fair*, and the Bad Sex column in *Nerve.com*. His short stories have appeared in numerous anthologies and *The Mississippi Review*. He lives somewhere in the world with his wife and son, but it's hard to say where, exactly, because he moves often.

Scott Pomfret is co-author of the Romentics-brand line of romance novels for gay men (www.romentics.com). His short stories have been published in *Post Road, New Delta Review, Genre Magazine, Freshmen: Best New Gay Voices, Best GayErotica 2005*, and many other magazines and anthologies. Pomfret has just completed the Great Gay Catholic American Novel, *Only Say the Word.*

Matthue Roth lives in California. His first novel, *Never Mind the Goldbergs*, was published by Scholastic in January 2005, and his second, tentatively called *Revival*, will be published by Cleis Press in September. He has filmed for HBO's *Def Poetry Jam* and *Rock the Vote*, and has appeared in the National Queer Arts Festival and the Cannes Film Festival. He keeps a secret online journal at www.matthue.com.

Kevin Sampsell lives in Portland, Oregon, and is the publisher of the influential micropress Future Tense Books. He is the editor of *The Insomniac Reader: Stories of the Night* (Manic D Press) and the author of many small books including *Beautiful Blemish* (Word Riot Press).

Lori Selke has not done your girlfriend backstage; she has not spanked her over the bar or felt her up in an alley. But she'll consider it if you ask nicely. She is the editor of *Tough Girls: Down and Dirty Dyke Erotica* and the little lit zine *Problem Child*. You can find more of her fiction in *Bottoms Up, Ultimate Lesbian Erotica*, and *Dyke the Halls*, among other places.

Despite her penchant for sex, risky fiction, and midnight walks, *Heather Shaw* is just a nice girl from Indiana now living in the San Francisco Bay Area. Her fiction has appeared in cool places such as *Polyphony* and *Strange Horizons*, and she co-edits *Flytrap*, the little zine with teeth, with her fiancé Tim Pratt. Her day job, buying books for the catalog *Blowfish* and editing their erotica webzine (www.fishnetmag.com), is pretty cool, too. While not working on her novel, she enjoys dancing, cats (but not dancing with cats), gardening and mangos. Her web presence begins at www.hlshaw.com.

Felicia Sullivan is a New York based writer with an MFA from Columbia University. A two-time Pushcart Prize nominee, her work has been published in *Post Road Magazine, Drunken Boat, Publishers Weekly*, and *The Adirondack Review*, among other publications. Work is forthcoming in *Swink Magazine, the anthology*, and *Kitchen Sink*. She is the founder and editor of the literary journal, Small Spiral Notebook (www.smallspiralnotebook.com), and is also the director of the nonfiction series at KGB Bar in NYC. Felicia is at work on a memoir and a novel.

Phil West is a writer currently living and working in San Antonio. He curates the puro ¡SLAM! poetry slam series, the best-attended weekly poetry reading in the state of Texas, and teaches at San Antonio College and Our Lady of the Lake University. He is also at work co-editing an oral history of poetry slam, to be published by Soft Skull Press, and his first book of poetry, *The Arsenal of Small Stars,* is due out in early 2005 from Orchard Press.

San Francisco-based poet *Daphne Gottlieb* stitches together the ivory tower and the gutter just using her tongue. She is the author of three books of poetry: *Final Girl* (2003), *Why Things Burn* (2001) and *Pelt* (1999). She was the winner of the 2003 Audre Lorde Award for Poetry and a 2001 Firecracker Alternative Book Award. She is the poetry editor for *Other* magazine and *Lodestar Quarterly* and her work frequently appears in journals and anthologies, including *Nerve.com*, *Mcsweeneys.net*, *Red Light: Superheroes, Saints and Sluts*, *With a Rough Tongue*, and *Bullets and Butterflies*. You can find her online at www.daphnegottlieb.com. She is currently at work on her fourth book tentatively entitled *Kissing Dead Girls*, and has never, to her knowledge, wrecked a home.